The Great Ice Cream Book

The Great Ice Cream Book

A wonderful collection of recipes
for ice creams and sorbets
from the finest restaurants
in Great Britain and Ireland

Absolute Press

Published by Absolute Press (publishers)
14 Widcombe Crescent, Widcombe Hill, Bath, Avon.

First published July 1984

© Absolute Press (publishers)

Editors
Robin Edwards
Jon Croft

Illustrations
Joe Mallia

Cover Photograph
Michael Standard

Printed by
Photobooks (Bristol) Limited, Barton Manor,
St. Philips, Bristol

Contents

Introduction

Everyone loves ice cream. It is a universal food that is fun and that can be enjoyed at almost any time of the day, in summer or in winter. It will surprise some people to discover that restaurants find little variance in requests for ice creams and sorbets from one season to the next.

The history of ice creams and water ices is a long one. It is generally believed to be the Chinese who developed the art of making iced sweets. About 10 centuries ago they used to chill their fruit and tea drinks with ice, and it was from these early experiments that the fruit flavoured ices first appeared. The Chinese taught the art of making iced sweets to the Indians, Persians and Arabs. In Europe the iced sweet first made an appearance in renaissance times in Italy, in the form of a *sorbetto.* It was the great chefs of Italy who first realised the gastronomic potentials of ice creams and water ices and who introduced the art to the French. Throughout the 18th and 19th centuries ices became very fashionable and with the developments in refrigeration in the 20th century it became possible for everyone to make ice creams.

The Great Ice Cream Book will enable everyone to make stunning iced sweets, using fresh garden produce, flavourings such as coffee and ginger and of course the countless varieties of liqueurs and spirits. All you need is a freezer compartment and you will be making ice creams and sorbets just like those that grace the tables of many of the finest restaurants in Great Britain and Ireland. All the recipes in this book have been gathered from the kitchens of the very best restaurants, the chefs of which have generously and enthusiastically given up much of their valuable time in order to contribute to the book.

The Great Ice Cream Book will help you to discover a whole new world of exotic flavours and tastes—but be careful, eating ice cream can be habit forming!

Ice Creams

Amaretto and Praline Ice Cream

No 3, Glastonbury
Chef/proprietor Jillian Gilliat

8 egg yolks
8 oz. (225g.) castor sugar
1 pint (575ml.) double cream
4 tablespoons Amaretto
equal quantities unblanched
    almonds and sugar to make
    3 oz. (75g.) praline
small macaroons for garnish

Make the praline by caramelising the almonds and sugar in a heavy pan. Turn out onto an oiled marble surface and allow to get cold. When cold, reduce to a powder.

Beat the yolks with the sugar in a bowl over hot, but not boiling, water until white and creamy. Add the cream gradually and continue beating so that the mixture remains thick and fluffy. Drip in the Amaretto while still beating. Fold in the praline.

Place into freezer. This ice cream will need no further stirring. Serve with small macaroons and a dash of Amaretto.

Apple Mint Ice Cream

Hope End, Ledbury
Chef/proprietor Patricia Hegarty

Serves 8

3–4 good handfuls fresh apple
   mint leaves—apple mint
   retains the best colour
1 lb. (450g.) sugar
1 pint (575ml.) water
juice 3 lemons
1 pint (575ml.) double cream
Crème de Menthe, for garnish

Make a syrup by dissolving the sugar in the water. Boil for three or four minutes and leave to cool.

Put the mint leaves into a liquidiser, add the syrup and whizz. Press the bright green juice very thoroughly through a nylon sieve. Add the juice of the lemons.

Freeze in a shallow metal tray until a thick slush has formed. Process again and fold in the whipped cream. Freeze again in a covered container for 3–4 hours.

Decorate with fresh sprigs of mint or angelica. For a special occasion, outline each serving with a trickle of Crème de Menthe.

Apple and Raisin Ice Cream with Cinnamon Sauce

Lichfield's, Richmond
Chef/proprietor Stephen Bull

Serves 6–8

For the ice cream:

4 egg yolks
2 oz. (50g.) castor sugar
½ pint (275ml.) single cream

For the apple mixture:

1½ lb. (675g.) Bramleys,
    peeled, cored and roughly
    chopped
juice and grated rind 1 orange
2 oz. (50g.) castor sugar
Calvados or cider
2 oz. (50g.) raisins

For the sauce:

4 tablespoons golden syrup
2 sticks cinnamon
2 cloves
½" lemon peel
lemon juice

It is important to remember in this recipe, when you are adding the sugar to the apples, that Bramleys vary in tartness and may need more or less than the 2 oz. (50g.) suggested.

To make the ice cream, whisk together the egg yolks and sugar in a heavy pan. Heat the cream to simmering and slowly pour onto the egg mixture, whisking constantly. Cook over a medium heat until the custard coats the back of a spoon, whisking all the time. Do not boil. Remove from heat and cool.

Place the apples in a heavy pan, add the juice and rind of the orange, the castor sugar and cook over a low heat until the apples form a dryish purée. While they are cooking, heat some Calvados or cider and soak the raisins in it until plump. When the purée and raisins have cooled, combine with the custard and freeze for 4 hours. Remove once or twice as the mixture solidifies and mix well.

Make the sauce by heating the golden syrup in ½ pint (275ml.) water. Infuse the resulting mixture with the cinnamon, cloves and the lemon peel. Reduce over gentle heat for about 20 minutes, add a few drops of lemon juice, strain and cool.

Apricot and Almond Ice Cream

Pool Court, Pool In Wharfdale
Chef Melvyn Jordan

Serves 6

2 lb. (900g.) dried apricots
juice ½ lemon
4 egg yolks
½ pint (275ml.) double cream
6 oz. (175g.) castor sugar
4 oz. (125g.) almond biscuits
   (amaretti, macaroon or
   ratafia)

Soak the apricots overnight. Pour off the water and cook in fresh water for about 25 minutes. Allow to cool. Liquidise.

In a clean pan put the yolks, sugar and cream and apricot pulp. Place over low flame and stir continuously. When the mixture begins to thicken (do not boil) take off heat and immediately pour through a sieve. Add the lemon juice and allow to cool.

After about 2 hours freeze either way as follows: if using deep freeze, place into a bowl and put into freezer, stirring from the sides to the middle every 15 minutes or so: if using an ice cream machine just follow manufacturers instructions.

When just about set, crush biscuits and fold in.

Baileys Ice Cream

Le Coq Hardi, Dublin
Chef/proprietor John Howard

6 egg yolks
6 oz. (175g.) castor sugar
3 tablespoons Baileys Irish
   Cream Liqueur
7 fl.oz. (200ml.) double cream
chopped hazelnuts
chopped raisins

This recipe can also be very successful if using Irish Mist Liqueur instead of Baileys.

Melt 5 oz. (150g.) of the sugar with a few tablespoons of water. Boil and keep the syrup hot.

Put the egg yolks into a large bowl, pour in the warm syrup and whisk the mixture over a bowl of hot water until it begins to thicken. Take off the heat and continue to whisk until cold.

Whip the cream with 1 oz. (25g.) of sugar until light and fluffy. Fold together the egg mixture and whipped cream, making sure that they have combined well. Place in ice cream machine or deep freeze. When partly frozen stir in the raisins and nuts. Finish freezing.

Bananas Double

Chez Moi, London W11
Chef/proprietor Richard Walton

1 lb. (450g.) very ripe bananas, peeled
1 lemon
3 drops almond essence
1 pint (575ml.) double cream
2 fl.oz. (50ml.) glycerine
4 eggs
4 oz. (125g.) sugar

For the bananas en papillote:

1 large not too ripe banana, per person
1 tablespoon rum or brandy, per person
1 tablespoon melted apricot jam, per person
1 teaspoon melted butter, per person

To make the ice cream, liquidise the bananas with the rind and juice from the lemon.

Boil the sugar with a teacup of water until softball on the thermometer.

Whisk the cream, as it starts to thicken add the glycerine and the banana purée, continue to whisk till thick.

Pour the sugar syrup onto the eggs and whisk till thick and creamy and cool. Fold into the cream mixture. Place into ice cream machine or deep freeze.

To make the bananas en papillote, preheat the oven to 425F/220C/gas 7. Place the bananas on tin foil and pour the brandy, jam and butter over. Seal and cook for 10–15 minutes. To serve, cut the bananas into 3 and place around a scoop of the ice cream. Pour over sauce and serve on lightly warmed plates.

Biscuit aux Noisettes au Coulis de Framboises

Lichfield's, Richmond
Chef/proprietor Stephen Bull

For the ice cream:

8 egg yolks
1 pint (575ml.) single cream
2 oz. (50g.) castor sugar

For the sauce:

1 punnet raspberries
1–2 tablespoons sugar syrup
little lemon juice
Eau de Vie de Framboise or
    Liqueur de Framboise,
    if available

For the praline:

6 oz. (175g.) hazelnuts
6 oz. (175g.) sugar
3 tablespoons water

Make the ice cream by beating the yolks and sugar in a heavy enamel pan until creamy and thick. Meanwhile, bring the cream to the boil and whisking constantly pour into the egg yolk mixture. Place pan over moderate heat and whisk until the mixture has thickened so that it coats the back of a spoon. Leave to cool.

Make the praline by toasting the hazelnuts in a hot oven for 5 minutes. Rub off the skins between two tea towels and crush roughly in the food processor. Return to the oven to toast to a golden brown. In a saucepan melt the sugar with the water until it starts to turn brown, add the nuts and stir until all is toffee-coloured. Pour onto an oiled surface and let get cold. Then pound or crush in the food processor. Add to the cold ice cream mixture.

Freeze the ice cream in a loaf tin, stirring once or twice. Remove from mould and cut into slices and surround with a raspberry sauce.

To make the sauce, pour the raspberries into the liquidiser add the sugar syrup and a little lemon juice and if you have any, the Eau de Vie de Framboise. Liquidise for 20 seconds and then pass through a sieve.

Bistro Brown Bread Ice Cream

Bistro Nine, Colchester
Chef/proprietor Penny Campbell

8 oz. (225g.) coarse brown
   breadcrumbs
8 oz. (225g.) demerara sugar
2 pints cream (generous litre)
   lightly whipped
brandy to taste

We make our own bread at the Bistro, made with a mixture of fine and coarse organic brown flour. I suppose the equivalent would be a wholewheat bread.

Thoroughly mix together the breadcrumbs and sugar. Carefully brown in a hot oven, stirring so that they become evenly brown and crisp. They need to be quite brown but be sure not to burn them as this makes the ice cream bitter.

Allow the crumbs to cool and then crush with a pestle and mortar.

Stir in the crumbs and a good few slurps of brandy to the lightly whipped cream—the brandy will help stop the ice cream from freezing too solid.

Place into ice cream machine or deep freeze. Remove from freezer 15 minutes before serving.

Blackcurrant Ice Cream

Cleeveway House, Bishops Cleeve
Chef/proprietor John Marfell

Serves 8

4 eggs, separated
½ lb. (225g.) castor sugar
1 pint (575ml.) double cream
12 oz. (350g.) blackcurrants

Stew and sieve the blackcurrants to make a purée. Allow to cool.

Whip up the cream to soft peaks and whip in the egg yolks. Combine with the purée.

Whip up the egg whites with the sugar and fold this meringue mixture into the fruit and cream. Place into ice cream machine or deep freeze. If using a deep freeze, bring out from time to time and stir.

Glace de Cannenberge

Chez Moi, London W11
Chef/proprietor Richard Walton

Serves 6

2 x 7 oz. (200g.) punnets
  Ocean Spray fresh
  cranberries
½ pint (275ml.) rosé wine
½ pint (275ml.) red wine
6 oz. (175ml.) sugar
1 cinnamon stick
8 cloves
3 thick slices lemon
3 thick slices orange
2 drops vanilla essence
1 good dash Angostura Bitters
¼ pint (150ml.) glycerine
½ pint (275ml.) double cream
3 egg yolks

Make the syrup by reducing the wines with the sugar, cinnamon, cloves, vanilla, bitters, glycerine, orange and lemon slices till 'jam' on cooking thermometer.

Strain the syrup onto the picked over berries and bring back to the boil until the berries start to pop. Allow to cool and refrigerate.

Whisk the cream until it starts to thicken, then slowly add berries and syrup and whisk till thick. Whisk the egg yolks separately and fold in. Freeze. The ice cream can be made lighter by also folding in the whisked egg whites at the end, though it is not necessary.

Caramel Ice Cream

Chez Nico, London SW8
Chef/proprietor Nico Ladenis

6 egg yolks
12 oz. (350g.) sugar
11 fl.oz. (300ml.) cream
11 fl.oz. (300ml.) milk
vanilla pod

Melt the sugar in a small heavy pan, along with the vanilla pod, without adding a drop of water. Do not let the caramel get too brown and bitter. Keep stirring until you achieve a completely melted effect.

Let the cream come to the boil and add the caramel with great care to avoid splashing or even burning yourself.

Put the eggs in a mixing bowl and whip well. Bring the milk to the boil and pour gradually over the whipped eggs, whisking all the time. Combine this mixture with the caramel and cream mixture and stir well. Cook for 5 minutes over a low heat stirring all the time. Remove vanilla pod and allow to cool completely. Place into an ice-cream machine or domestic ice cream churner to complete.

Bombe Chartreuse

The Peat Inn, Peat Inn, Fife
Chef/proprietor David Wilson

Serves 6

12 egg yolks
8 oz. (225g.) granulated sugar
8 fl.oz. (225ml.) cold water
15 fl.oz. (425ml.) double cream
2 fl.oz. (50ml.) Green
  Chartreuse
little green food colouring
strawberries or raspberries,
  puréed for a sauce

Bring the water and sugar to the boil and cook for 5 minutes.

Beat the egg yolks until pale and fluffy. Add the syrup to the egg yolks. Transfer to a double boiler or into a heavy based pan inside a larger pan with a little water in. Heat until the mixture is thick enough to coat the back of a spoon, stirring all the time. Allow to cool.

When cool add the cream, the Green Chartreuse and food colouring. Place into the ice cream machine or deep freeze until ready. If using the deep freeze, bring out from time to time and stir.

For serving, put the mixture into a bombe mould or individual moulds (a tea cup will do). Place in freezer, covered in cling film, until required. To serve, reverse out onto the plate and surround with strawberry or raspberry purée. Garnish the top of the bombe with a fresh mint leaf.

Chocolate and Chestnut Ice Cream

Hope End, Ledbury
Chef/proprietor Patricia Hegarty

For the custard base:

2 eggs
2 egg yolks
3 oz. (75g.) muscovado sugar
1 pint (575ml.) milk
5 fl.oz. (150ml.) double cream,
  whipped

8 oz. (225g.) dried chestnuts
2 good tablespoons honey
vanilla pod
6 oz. (175g.) best bitter
  chocolate

Cover the chestnuts with water and simmer with the vanilla pod until the chestnuts are tender, about 2 hours. Add a little water if the chestnuts seem to be drying out. Cool slightly and whizz in blender, adding enough cooking liquor to make a purée.

Make the custard by beating the eggs and sugar in a bowl. Heat the milk until it is almost at boiling point and pour over the egg mixture. Return to the pan and cook carefully over a very low heat, whisking all the time, until the mixture thickens enough to coat the back of a spoon. Do not boil. Remove from heat, cool and fold in the whipped cream.

Melt the chocolate in a bowl over a saucepan of hot water. Combine the chocolate, chestnut purée and custard. Freeze in an ice cream machine or in a plastic container with a lid. To serve, decorate with grated chocolate, crystallised violets or, if you are feeling extravagant, crumbled marron glacé.

Chocolate and Coffee Ice Cream

Carved Angel, Dartmouth
Chef/proprietor Joyce Molyneux

Serves 6–8

8 oz. (225g.) Menier chocolate
3 oz. (75g.) ground coffee
½ pint (275ml.) milk
8 oz. (225g.) sugar
5 fl.oz. (150ml.) egg white
15 fl.oz. (425ml.) double cream

Put the coffee in the milk and bring to the boil and infuse for 15 minutes. Strain through a muslin over chocolate broken into pieces. Mix till smooth.

Cook the sugar and egg whites over hot water to make a meringue. Remove from heat and beat till cool.

Whip the cream lightly.

When the chocolate mixture and meringue are cool, fold into the cream carefully. This mixture can be placed into a container and frozen without churning or piped into meringue cases and frozen. Serves well straight from the freezer.

Parfait au Chocolat Praliné

La Potinière, Gullane
Chef/proprietor Hilary Brown

4 oz. (125g.) Bournville
   plain chocolate
2 oz. (50g.) castor sugar
4 tablespoons cold water
½ pint (275ml.) double cream
3 large egg yolks (size 2)
2 tablespoons dark rum

For the praline:

2 oz. (50g.) almonds,
   unblanched
2 oz. (50g.) castor sugar

Make the praline by melting the sugar in a heavy pan. Cook until golden brown, add the almonds and stir together. Pour onto a lightly buttered baking tray. When cold, crush coarsely in a processor.

Break the chocolate into a processor.

Place the sugar and water in a small pan. Dissolve the sugar and then bring to the boil. Boil for about 5 minutes until 4 tablespoons of syrup are left.

While the syrup is boiling, add the rum to the cream and whip until it forms soft peaks.

Pour the syrup onto the chocolate, cover and blend for 30 seconds. Drop in the yolks and continue to blend until thick and paler. Empty the mixture onto the cream and using a balloon whisk, gently mix together until thoroughly blended. Mix in 2 oz. (50g.) of the praline.

Transfer to 6–8 'pot au crème' dishes. Freeze for at least 3 hours. Take out a few minutes before serving, top with a swirl of whipped cream and sprinkle with a little crushed praline.

Parfait au Chocolat, Sauce Café

Priory Hotel, Bath
Chef Mike Collom

Serves 8

1 lb. (450g.) plain chocolate
½ pint (275ml.) double cream,
  half whipped
5 fl.oz. (150ml.) single cream
4 eggs
4 oz. (125g.) castor sugar
2 tablespoons rum

For the sauce:

4 egg yolks
½ pint (275ml.) single cream
1 teaspoon instant coffee
1 tablespoon Tia Maria
2 oz. (50g.) castor sugar

Make the parfait by melting the chocolate in a saucepan which is standing in hot water.

Whip the eggs and sugar until light and fluffy. To this, quickly add the melted chocolate and then fold in the half-whipped cream and then lastly the rum. Pour into a tin foil lined terrine mould. Place into deep freeze for 24 hours.

Make the sauce by whisking the egg yolks and sugar together. Bring the cream to the boil and pour onto the beaten yolks and sugar, whisking all the time. Still whisking, return to the pan and heat gently until the mixture thickens and coats the back of the spoon. Do not boil. Dissolve the instant coffee in the Tia Maria and add to the custard and allow to cool.

To serve, pour the coffee sauce on individual plates and then slice the parfait and lay on top. Decorate with whipped cream and any colourful fruit and a crisp biscuit.

Cinnamon Ice Cream

Pool Court, Pool In Wharfdale
Chef Melvyn Jordan

1 pint (575ml.) milk
6 whole cinnamon sticks
1 oz. (25g.) glucose
4 oz. (125g.) sugar
4 oz. (125g.) egg yolks (approx.
    6 depending on size)
½ teaspoon ground cinnamon
5 fl.oz. (150ml.) double cream

Place the cinnamon sticks in the milk and bring to the boil. Allow to cool, about 4 hours.

Beat the egg yolks with the sugar and strain the cold milk. Whisk the milk and egg yolks together and add the glucose. Place the mixture into a thick bottomed pan and put on a moderate heat, stirring continuously till the mixture coats the back of a spoon—do not boil. Strain into a bowl and stir in the ground cinnamon and double cream. Allow to go cold and freeze.

Place mixture into ice cream machine or deep freeze. If using a deep freeze, place mixture into a sealed plastic container and put into deep freeze. Stir from the edges to the middle at 20 minute intervals. Beat the mixture vigorously when it starts to thicken. When ice cream is ready, store in a sealed plastic container.

Coconut Ice Cream with Fresh Mango

Beechfield House, Beanacre
Chef/proprietor Peter Crawford-Rolt

Serves 8

8 egg yolks
11 oz. (300g.) castor sugar
1 pint (575ml.) milk
1 pint (575ml.) cream
1 x 15 oz. (425g.) tin
   Cream of Coconut
8 mangoes
toasted dessicated coconut for
   garnish

Bring the milk and cream to the boil.

Whisk the sugar and egg yolks together and whisk into the just boiled milk and cream. Return to a gentle heat, stirring constantly, until the custard coats the back of a wooden spoon. Allow to cool and stir in the can of Cream of Coconut. Place into ice cream machine or deep freeze. If using deep freeze, bring out from time to time and stir.

To serve, cut the mangoes in half, either side of the stone, and carefully cut the flesh out from the halves with a grapefruit knife, keeping the skin intact. Scoop the ice cream into the empty skins and sprinkle with the dessicated coconut. Slice the mango flesh and arrange in a fan around the ice cream.

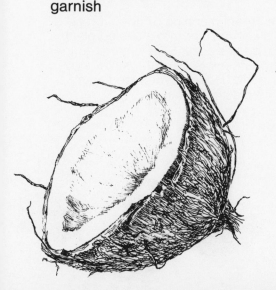

Coffee and Hazelnut Ice Cream

Country Elephant, Painswick
Chef/proprietor Jane Medforth

Serves 8

6 eggs, separated
½ pint (275ml.) double cream
6 oz. (175ml.) castor sugar
6 oz. (75g.) hazelnuts, shelled, toasted and chopped
2 dessertspoons Camp coffee essence

Whisk the egg yolks and cream together until thick. Add the coffee essence.

Whisk the egg whites until stiff and slowly whisk in the sugar. Fold the two mixtures together with the chopped nuts and freeze. This ice cream can be served straight from the freezer.

Iced Coffee Soufflé

The Priory, Bath
Chef, Mike Collom

Serves 8

1½ pints (875ml.) double
   cream
4 eggs
4 egg yolks
6 oz. (175ml.) castor sugar
4 teaspoons instant coffee
4 tablespoons Tia Maria
icing sugar and powdered
   coffee

This sweet is best done in individual soufflé dishes. Prepare these by lining with double thickness greaseproof paper, so that the paper comes 1" (2cm.) above the rim of the dish. This is so that when you remove the paper the frozen mixture will be in the shape of a soufflé.

Dissolve the instant coffee in a tablespoon of boiling water. Allow to cool and then add 1 pint (575ml.) of the double cream and half of the Tia Maria. Lightly whip, it must not be stiff.

Whisk the eggs, egg yolks and sugar until very light and fluffy. Very carefully fold this mixture into the lightly whipped cream. Pour into the prepared moulds and deep freeze for 6–8 hours.

To serve, whip up the remaining cream for piping. Remove the paper from the soufflés by dipping the dish in warm water. Using a grapefruit knife, hollow out the middle and put to one side. Pour the remaining Tia Maria into the hollow and pipe with the whipped cream. Replace the hollowed out piece and dust with a mixture of icing sugar and powdered coffee. Serve at once.

Cointreau Ice Cream

Blostin's, Shepton Mallet
Chef/proprietor Bill Austin

½ lb. (225g.) castor sugar
6 egg yolks
1 pint (575ml.) double cream
finely grated zest of 1 orange
3 fl.oz. (75ml.) Cointreau

Cream the egg yolks and sugar to the ribbon stage. Add the Cointreau and the zest.

Lightly whip the cream and fold into the egg mixture with a metal spoon.

Place in freezer to cool overnight. After one hour in the freezer, remove and stir and replace. The ice cream will be able to be scooped straight from the freezer into serving bowls when required. Decorate with bits of orange peel.

Cranberry Swirl Ice Cream

Bodysgallen Hall, Llandudno
Chef, David Harding

For the vanilla ice cream:

4 whole eggs
4 yolks
4 oz. (125g.) sugar
1 pint (575ml.) milk
1 vanilla pod
1 pint (575ml.) double cream,
  partially whipped

8 oz. (225g.) cranberries
6 oz. (175g.) castor sugar
2 tablespoons water
zest of ½ lemon

Make the ice cream, by beating the eggs, yolks and sugar together till well blended.

Split the vanilla pod and add to the milk. Infuse the pod in the milk in a double boiler, covered, for about 10 minutes.

Strain the mixture onto the eggs, mix, and return to pan. Cook till thick and creamy. Strain into a bowl and whisk until it cools. When cool add the cream. Allow to get cold and place into ice cream machine or deep freeze. If using the deep freeze, bring out from time to time and stir.

Boil the cranberries, sugar and water until they pop. Add the lemon zest and cool. If using an ice cream machine, when virtually frozen, add the purée and give one or two churns and place into a plastic container. If using deep freeze you will have to get the swirl effect by hand and hard work!

Iced Drambuie Parfait

The Old Monastery, Drybridge
Chef/proprietor Douglas Craig

7 oz. (200g.) granulated sugar
5 fl.oz. (150ml.) water
4 eggs, separated
4 tablespoons Drambuie
2 oz. (50g.) icing sugar
½ pint (275ml.) double cream

This dessert will keep for weeks and is very useful for unexpected guests!

Place 8 large wine glasses or sundae dishes into the freezer.

Dissolve the granulated sugar in the water and boil rapidly until the mixture is just turning golden—about 5 minutes. Remove from heat.

Beat the egg yolks and add the syrup, beating all the time. Continue to beat until the mixture cools and is light and fluffy—about 7 minutes. Beat in the Drambuie slowly. Chill thoroughly.

Whisk 2 of the egg whites until stiff. Whisk in the icing sugar and beat until stiff again.

Lightly whip the cream and fold into the Drambuie mixture, followed by the meringue mixture. Pile into glasses, cover and freeze. (It may be necessary to beat the Drambuie before folding in the cream and meringue.) Serve direct from the freezer and accompany with homemade shortbread or brandy snaps.

Glace de Freezomint

Mallory Court, Bishops Tachbrook
Chef Allan Holland

Serves 8–10

1 pint (575ml.) double cream
pinch salt
½ teaspoon vanilla essence
4 egg yolks
12 egg whites
10 fl.oz. (275ml.) Crème de
   Menthe
8 oz. (225g.) good quality plain
   chocolate

Roughly chop the chocolate and sieve so that you are left with small pieces of chocolate about the size of a pea. Set aside.

Whip the cream, salt, vanilla essence and egg yolks until the mixture begins to thicken. Slowly add the Crème de Menthe and continue whisking until thick.

Whisk the egg whites till stiff and fold into the cream mixture. Freeze.

When the mixture is almost frozen, stir in the chocolate and put in the freezer.

Fromage Glacé aux Pruneaux et à l'Armagnac

Mijanou, London SW1
Chef/proprietor Sonia Blech

Serves 8

9 oz. (250g.) best quality new
   season prunes, pipped
4 oz. (125g.) 0% fat fromage
   blanc or curd cheese
7 fl.oz. (200ml.) Crème
   Chantilly
juice and rind 1 orange
4 fl.oz. (125ml.) Armagnac
1 Earl Grey tea bag
4 oz. (125g.) sugar

Soak overnight the prunes in the orange juice and rind, Armagnac, the tea bag and enough boiling water to cover.

Next day weigh 7 oz. (200g.) of prunes and put aside the rest for garnish.

Strain the liquid and add the sugar. Cook on a slow heat until it is very, very tight and caramelises just at the edges (no more). Add this liquid, the cheese and the prunes into a food processor and work just enough to mix evenly. Leave to cool well.

Fold the Crème Chantilly very carefully into the cold prune mixture. Freeze in individual glasses or in a container. Serve with the rest of the soaked prunes as garnish and sprinkle with a little more Armagnac.

Fruit Cake Ice Cream

Billesley Manor, Stratford-Upon-Avon
Chef Ian Whittock

Serves 8

½ pint (275ml.) double cream
½ pint (275ml.) milk
4 egg yolks
1 oz. (25g.) ground almonds
2 oz. (50g.) castor sugar
3–4 oz. (75–125g.) fruit cake,
   finely chopped
2 fl.oz. (50ml.) brandy

Bring the milk and the cream just to the boil.

Whisk together the egg yolks, sugar and almonds. Pour the hot milk and cream over the egg mixture and whisk. Return to a clean pan on the stove, stirring with a wooden spoon until it coats the back of the spoon—do not boil. Allow to cool.

When it has reached the correct consistency and has cooled, add the cake and brandy. Place into an ice cream machine or the deep freeze. If using the deep freeze, bring out from time to time and stir.

Ginger Ice Cream

Plough Inn, Fadmoor
Chef/proprietor Kath Brown

Serves 8–10

½ pint (275ml.) double cream
2 rounded tablespoons icing
  sugar
2 rounded tablespoons soft
  brown sugar
7 oz. (175g.) chopped stem
  ginger
2 tablespoons syrup from
  ginger jar
4 eggs, separated

Sieve the sugars.

Whip the cream with the sieved sugars until thick.

Mash up the yolks and mix with the ginger, and the syrup.
Fold into the cream.

Whip the egg whites till stiff and fold into the mixture.
Place in deep freeze.

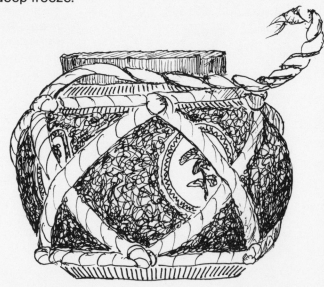

Ginger and Lychee Ice Cream

Ston Easton Park, Ston Easton
Chef Robert Jones

Serves 8–10

2 pints (generous litre) milk
10 egg yolks
6 oz. (175g.) sugar
3 drops vanilla
4 oz. (125g.) castor sugar
5 fl.oz. (150ml.) double cream
1 small jar stem ginger in
   syrup
1 small tin lychees
1½ oz. (40g.) ground ginger

Put the milk on to warm with the ground ginger.

Whisk the egg yolks, sugar and vanilla essence until almost white.

Whisk the milk into the eggs and sugar and pass through a fine sieve. Return to a clean pan and put onto a low heat and stir continuously until it coats the back of a spoon. Do not boil. Pass through a sieve and leave to go cold.

When cold add the double cream and some diced stem ginger and diced lychees to preference. Place into ice cream machine or deep freeze. If using deep freeze, bring out and stir every 15–20 minutes until set.

Frozen Ginger Meringue Cake

Croque-en-Bouche, Malvern Wells
Chefs/proprietors Robin and Marion Jones

Serves 8

1¼ pint (725ml.) double cream
1 tablespoon castor sugar
3 pieces stem ginger, finely
  chopped
1 tablespoon stem ginger
  syrup
1 tablespoon Kahlua (coffee
  liqueur)

For the coffee syrup:

2 tablespoons instant coffee
1 tablespoon sugar
1 tablespoon boiling water

For the meringues:

12 oz. (350g.) sugar
6 egg whites

Make the coffee syrup by mixing together all the ingredients until the sugar and coffee dissolve. Be sure to chill well.

Make crisp meringues and break into small pieces.

Whip the cream to the soft peak stage and mix in the sugar, Kahlua and half of the coffee syrup. Fold together the mixture with the chopped ginger, meringues and ginger syrup.

Fill a straight sided cake tin, lined with non-stick paper, (8" dia. x 2½" deep) with the mixture and marble the top with the remaining coffee syrup. Freeze for at least 24 hours before serving. The high sugar content will prevent the mixture from freezing too hard.

Gooseberry Ice Cream

Old Parsonage, Farrington Gurney
Chef/proprietor H. M. Gofton-Watson

2 lb. (900g.) gooseberries
8–10 oz. (225–275g.)
  granulated sugar
½ oz. (15g.) gelatine
5 tablespoons water
2 eggs
6 oz. (175g.) castor sugar
10 fl.oz. (275ml.) double cream,
  whipped

Heat the gooseberries slowly with the granulated sugar and cook until tender. Purée the mixture through a sieve and leave to cool.

Place one half of the purée in the deep freeze. Melt the gelatine in the water and add it to the remaining purée. Leave to cool.

Separate the eggs. Whip the whites until stiff and set aside. Beat the egg yolks with 2oz. (50g.) of the castor sugar until they are thick. Gradually add the cooled gelatine and fold in the whipped double cream. Place in the refrigerator.

When the frozen purée is nearly firm stir in the stiffly whipped egg whites and the remaining castor sugar. Then fold this mixture into the refrigerated one and place in the deep freeze. This ice cream will not require any further stirring.

Iced Grand Marnier Charlotte

Hunstrete House, Hunstrete
Chef Alain Dubois

3 oz. (75g.) castor sugar
grated rind and juice 2
   oranges
4 egg yolks
2 fl.oz. (50ml.) Grand Marnier
10 fl.oz. (275ml.) double cream,
   whipped
melted butter
20 boudoir biscuits

Line a 6″ Charlotte tin with the boudoir biscuits, having first dipped them in melted butter to ensure that they stick to the tin.

Combine the sugar, orange juice and rind in a saucepan. Bring to the boil for 3–4 minutes.

Place the yolks in an electric beater. Pour on the orange syrup, beating fast. Continue for 10 minutes. Add the Grand Marnier and beat. Lastly fold in the whipped cream and pour into the lined tin and chill in freezer.

To serve, run a pallette knife around the side of the tin and dip the tin briefly in hot water. Turn out and decorate with rosettes of cream.

Grand Marnier Ice Cream

Gidleigh Park, Chagford
Chef/proprietor Kay Henderson

Serves 6–8

6 egg yolks
½ lb. (175g.) sugar
1 tablespoon grated orange
   peel
3 fl.oz. (75ml.) water
1 pint (575ml.) double cream
3 tablespoons Grand Marnier

Whisk the egg yolks in an electric mixer until thick.

Bring the water, sugar and orange peel to the boil, stirring until the sugar dissolves. Boil briskly without stirring until the syrup reaches 230°.

Pour the hot syrup in a thin stream onto the egg yolks, whisking at high speed. Continue whisking for 10–15 minutes until the mixture becomes a thick, smooth cream. Add the Grand Marnier.

Whisk the cream until it is firm enough to form soft peaks. Fold the egg yolk mixture and cream together and put into ice cream machine or a covered container in the deep freeze.

Haselnuss-eis-Gugelhupf

Aval du Creux, Sark in the Channel Islands
Chef/proprietor Peter Hauser

Serves 8–10

6 egg yolks
6 oz. (175g.) icing sugar
18 fl.oz. (½ litre) double cream,
    whipped
2 oz. (50g.) raisins
5 oz. (150g.) chocolate ice
    cream (see page 00)
1 tablespoon hazelnut liqueur
6 tablespoons roasted
    almonds
little cocao powder

Cream the egg yolks and the icing sugar together and fold into the whipped cream and hazelnut liqueur.

Place half of the mixture in a Gugelhupf mould and freeze for 2 hours.

Remove from deep freeze and sprinkle over the mixture the raisins and the almonds. Put the ice cream on top and then cover with the rest of the cream mixture. Cover the dish with foil and keep in the deep freeze for 12 hours.

When required, turn out, sprinkle with cocao, garnish with a little tangy fruit and a leaf of lemon geranium, if available.

Honey and Cognac Ice Cream

Pomegranates, London SW1
Chef/proprietor Patrick Gwynn-Jones

Serves 12

6 eggs
½ lb. (225g.) clear honey
brandy—fill the ½ lb. jar
½ lb. (225g.) icing sugar
¾ pint (425ml.) double cream

Separate the eggs into different bowls. Whisk the whites until stiff. Add the icing sugar and whisk until very white and stiff.

In another bowl combine the beaten egg yolks, jar of honey and the 'honey jar' measure of brandy. Add to the stiff whites and blend. Add the cream and blend all together. Freeze for 2–3 hours. Remix and set to freeze again. Serve with Langue de Chat biscuits.

Honey and Walnut Ice Cream

Arbutus Lodge, Cork
Chef/proprietor Declan Ryan

Serves 8

18 fl.oz. (500ml.) milk
3½ oz. (100g.) sugar
6 egg yolks
9 fl.oz. (250ml.) whipping
  cream
3½ oz. (100g.) French walnuts,
  roughly chopped
honey to taste

Beat the egg yolks and sugar till white.

Put the honey and milk in a pan and bring to the boil. Check the milk for taste—you want the honey flavour to come through, neither too strong nor too weak.

Add some of the hot milk/honey mixture to the egg yolks, stirring constantly. Return to the stove with the rest of the milk and continue to cook over a low heat, stirring all the time, until the mixture coats the back of a spoon.

Allow to cool. When cooling, add the chopped walnuts.

Put into an ice cream machine or deep freeze. When partly frozen add the cream. If using a deep freeze, stir once or twice when the mixture thickens.

Kirsch Ice Cream with Red Summer Fruits

Cromlix House, Dunblane
Chef Mark Napper

4 oz. (125g.) each fresh
strawberries, raspberries,
redcurrants and stoned fresh
cherries

For the ice cream:

4 oz. (125g.) castor sugar
4 egg yolks
½ pint (275ml.) milk
½ pint (275ml.) double cream
5 fl.oz. (150ml.) Kirsch

For the tuile:

3 egg whites
4 oz. (125g.) castor sugar
2 oz. (50g.) plain flour
2 oz. (50g.) melted butter

Marinate the red fruits in a little Kirsch.

Make the ice cream by beating the egg yolks and sugar together. Bring the milk to just boiling point and pour over the egg mixture, stirring continuously, until it thickens enough to coat the back of a spoon. Do not boil. Cool completely and stir in the cream and Kirsch. Pour into ice cream machine or deep freeze. If using a deep freeze, bring out from time to time and stir.

Make the tuile by lightly whisking the egg whites and sugar. Beat in flour and then butter until it forms a just pourable batter. Form 6 dessertspoons of batter into 3″ rounds. Bake in a moderate oven for a few minutes until golden brown. Remove from tray and mold each one over the back of 1 lb. (450g.) jars to form tulip shapes.

To serve, fill each tulip with ice cream and top with fruits. To finish spin sugar over each one and serve immediately.

Lemon and Almond Ice Cream

The Rafters, Stow on the Wold
Chef/proprietor Keith Maby

Serves 10

1½ pints (850ml.) cream, stiffly
   whipped
1 lb. (450g.) castor sugar
juice and grated rind of 5
   medium lemons
4 oz. (100g.) lightly toasted
   and flaked almonds

For the custard:

12 egg yolks
5 oz. (150g.) castor sugar
1½ pints (850ml.) single cream

Whisk the egg yolks and sugar until thick and white.

Scald the single cream and add to the egg and sugar mixture. Return to stove over water and stir until custard coats the back of a spoon. Do not boil. Cool.

Add other ingredients and place in freezer until mixture begins to firm. Take out of freezer and place in rotary beater and whisk well. Refreeze.

Glace Malibu

Marlfield House, Gorey
Chef/proprietor Mary Bowe

Serves 10

11 oz. (300g.) sugar
12 egg yolks
2 pints (generous litre) milk
vanilla pod
3 measures Malibu cocktail
orange segments for garnish

In a heavy pan beat the sugar and egg yolks until white.

Infuse the vanilla pod in the milk and bring to just boiling. Pour carefully onto the egg mixture, whisking all the time. Return to heat and cook gently until the custard coats the back of a spoon, still whisking all the time. Do not boil. Strain and add the cream to halt the cooking process. Cool.

When cool add the Malibu and place into an ice cream machine or deep freeze. If using a deep freeze, bring out from time to time and stir well. Serve garnished with orange segments.

The Market Melon Ice Cream

The Market, Manchester
Chef/proprietor Lin Scrannage

1 ripe honeydew melon, about
   1 lb. (450g.) in flesh
4 oz. (125g.) castor sugar
juice 2 lemons
juice ½ lime
pinch ground ginger
2 measures Midori melon
   liqueur
8 fl.oz. (225g.) double cream

Cut the melon in half and remove the pips. Scoop out the flesh and liquidise to a purée. Make up to ½ pint (275ml.) with water.

Put into a pan with the sugar and heat to dissolve. Bring to the boil and boil rapidly for 2 minutes. Cool.

Add the lemon and lime juice, with the ginger and the Midori and pour into a plastic carton.

Place into ice cream machine or deep freeze. If using a deep freeze, bring out from time to time and stir. When mushy, beat the cream to soft peaks and fold in. Freeze again, stirring from time to time if using deep freeze.

To serve, put into refrigerator for about 45 minutes to soften. Serve in frosted glass dishes, green ones look good, with a generous spoonful of the Midori liqueur poured over.

Marmalade and Raspberry Millefeuille

Longueville Manor, Jersey
Chef John Dicken

Serves 8

5 oz. (150g.) homemade
   marmalade
3 oz. (75g.) sugar
5 fl.oz. (150ml.) water
15 fl.oz. (425ml.) cream, lightly
   whipped
3 eggs, separated
sugar syrup to taste

For the garnish:
8 oz. (225g.) puff pastry
1 lb. (450g.) raspberries
double cream, whipped

Line biscuit moulds with grease proof paper. Boil the sugar and water slowly until soft ball.

Whisk egg yolks over hot water until ribbon stage. Pour the sugar in slowly, whisking all the time. Remove from heat and beat till cold.

Work in marmalade and fold in the cream and the lightly whipped egg whites. Pour into biscuit moulds. Place in deep freeze for 24 hours.

Roll out puff pastry to 1/16" thick. Place on baking tray and prick all over with a fork. Rest for 30 minutes and bake until golden brown at 230°C/450°F/gas 8. Dust with icing sugar and glaze under grill quickly. Cool and cut into 2" x 3" rectangles.

Select 8 oz. (225g.) of the best raspberries. Liquidise the rest with the sugar syrup and pass through chinoise, removing pips.

Assemble dish by placing a strip of pastry on a plate, top with a slice of marmalade biscuit ice. Pipe a thin layer of cream over top. Arrange 12 good raspberries and piece of puff pastry on top. Surround with a ribbon of the raspberry coulis.

The Meringue and Chocolate Layer Cake

Horn of Plenty, Gulworthy
Chef/proprietor Sonia Stevenson

For the meringue:

10 oz. (275g.) castor sugar
5 egg whites

For the filling:

9 oz. (250g.) bitter chocolate
  (Menier)
9 teaspoons coffee powder
3 packets unsalted butter
14 oz. (400g.) icing sugar
5 egg whites

Make the meringue mixture in the usual manner. Make 4 or 5 sheets of thin meringue (4" x 8") and dry out on silicone paper. (You can use a circular cake base as an alternative shape.)

Make the filling mixture by putting the chocolate, coffee powder and 3 tablespoons of water in a saucepan and gently melt together. In a mixing bowl, cream the butter until soft and mix in the chocolate. In a double boiler put the egg whites and icing sugar and with an electric handbeater, whisk until hot and thick. Allow to cool a little and mix into the chocolate and butter mixture.

Layer the meringue sheets and the filling mixture alternately, finally covering the outside with the mixture completely. Chill in the freezer for a minimum of 2 hours. Remove 20 minutes or so before cutting into slices or wedges.

Mince Meat and Brandy Ice Cream

Cromlix House, Dunblane
Chef Mark Napper

4 oz. (125g.) castor sugar
4 egg yolks
½ pint (275ml.) milk
½ pint (275ml.) double cream
1 lb. (450g.) jar mince meat
5 fl.oz. (150ml.) brandy

This ice cream makes a rather delicious alternative to mince pies and Christmas pudding over the festive season.

Beat the egg yolks and sugar together. Bring the milk to just boiling point and pour over the mixture, beating continuously. Return custard mixture to the saucepan and stirring constantly with a wooden spoon, heat gently until the mixture thickens and coats the back of a spoon. Cool completely.

When cool, stir in the cream and brandy. Place into ice cream machine or deep freeze. If using a deep freeze, bring out from time to time and stir.

When just at freezing point, add mince meat and complete freezing.

Fluffy Mocha Ice Cream

Paul's, Folkestone
Chef/proprietor Paul Hagger

Serves 10

3 eggs
3 oz. (75g.) demerara sugar
2 fl.oz. (50ml.) coffee essence
  to taste
5½ oz. (160g.) good dark
  chocolate
1 pint (575ml.) double cream
1½ fl.oz. (40ml.) Tia Maria
grated chocolate or marzipan

Break the chocolate and melt over hot water in a small bowl. Keep warm.

Separate the eggs. Whip the egg yolks till stiff. Add the coffee essence gently with a hand whisk.

Whip the cream and sugar till light and fluffy. Fold in the cream to the yolks mixture.

In a perfectly clean bowl whip the egg whites till stiff but still smooth. Carefully fold into the yolk and cream mixture. Lightly fold in the warm chocolate to the mixture.

Give the empty bowls to somebody else to wash or to children to lick. Place into ice cream machine or deep freeze. Serve straight from the freezer decorated with grated chocolate or marzipan.

Glace Muscovite

Manley's, Storrington
Chef/proprietor Karl Löderer

Serves 8–10

1¾ pints (1 litre milk)
10 egg yolks
10 oz. (275g.) sugar
½ pint (275ml.) double cream
2 large measures Kummel

Bring the milk to the boil.

Cream the egg yolks and sugar in a bowl. Gently add the just boiled milk, stirring constantly, and re-heat gently until the mixture coats the back of a spoon. Do not boil.

Place in the refrigerator and then transfer to ice cream machine. Add the Kummel and double cream.

53

Nesserode Pudding

Wife of Bath, Wye
Chef/proprietor Bob Johnson

Serves 8

small tin chestnut purée
3 egg yolks
4 oz. (125g.) castor sugar
2 oz. (50g.) cornflour
5 fl.oz. (150ml.) milk
2 drops vanilla essence
1 bottle pure pineapple juice
2 leaves gelatine, softened in
   cold water
5 fl.oz. (150ml.) double cream
3 oz. (75g.) Menier chocolate

For the marinade:

2 oz. (50g.) mixed peel
zest 1 orange
zest 1 lemon
2 oz. (50g.) glace cherries
2 oz. (50g.) pistachio nuts
2 oz. (50g.) hazelnuts
brandy or Grand Marnier (or
   both)

Soak the chopped marinade ingredients in the liquor.

Soften the purée and place in Kenwood bowl with egg yolks and castor sugar. Whisk until a firm mixture is obtained. Add the cornflour and whisk in.

Scald the milk and vanilla essence and pour onto egg mixture. Return to heat and whisk until a thick custard. Do not boil. Allow to cool slightly.

Boil the pineapple juice and add the gelatine leaves and allow to cool. Whisk together the pineapple juice and the custard. Leave to cool.

Fold the marinade, liquor and all, into the mixture. Freeze until almost set. When almost set fold in the double cream and turn into a large basin and refrigerate until solid.

Place basin in warm water and then turn out pudding onto plate. Melt the chocolate in a bowl over hot water with a little butter. Spread thinly over gateau. Keep in freezer until 30 minutes before serving.

Orange and Caramel Bombe

Cooper's, Warminster
Chef/proprietor Frances Cooper

Serves 8

For the orange sorbet:

4 oz. (125g.) castor sugar
½ pint (275ml.) water
1 tablespoon lemon juice
grated rind 1 orange
grated rind 1 lemon
juice 3 oranges and 1 lemon, mixed
2 egg whites, whisked

For the caramel ice cream:

1 large tin condensed milk
1 pint (575ml.) single cream

For the garnish:

2 oranges, peeled and segmented
1 lb. (450g.) granulated sugar
6 fl.oz. (175ml.) water

To make the sorbet, dissolve the sugar in the water over a low heat. Bring to the boil and boil gently for 10 minutes. Add 1 tablespoon lemon juice. Put the rinds in a basin, pour over the boiling syrup and leave till cold. Add the juices and freeze. When half frozen, fold in the whisked egg whites. Continue freezing.

For the ice cream, stand the tin of condensed milk, unopened, in a pan of water and boil for 3 hours. The tin must be covered at all times by water. Cool. When cold, beat in single cream and freeze in the usual way.

Line individual bombe moulds with rounds of waxed paper, then with the ice cream. Make a hollow in the centre of the ice and fill with sorbet. Refreeze. Meanwhile make a syrup with the sugar and water. Boil until golden brown. Dip the segments or orange in the toffee and stand on oiled greaseproof paper to set. Dilute the remaining toffee with warm water for a light toffee sauce. To serve, invert bombes onto plates, surround with the toffee oranges and spoon a little sauce over.

Orange and Cardamom Ice Cream

Homewood Park, Hinton Charterhouse
Chef/proprietor Stephen Ross

Serves 8–10

For the custard:

8 egg yolks
8 oz. (225g.) sugar
1 pint (575ml.) milk

1 pint (575ml.) double cream,
   whipped
½ pint (275ml.) concentrated
   orange juice
2 teaspoons cardamom,
   ground

For this recipe try to use concentrated orange juice as it gives a much better result than fresh.

Bring the milk to the boil in a pan.

Meanwhile whisk the egg yolks and sugar together. Pour in the boiled milk and place over the heat, stirring until the mixture coats the back of a spoon. Allow to cool.

When cool, add the orange juice and cardamom and place into ice cream machine or deep freeze. When partly frozen beat in the whipped cream. If using a deep freeze, remove the mixture from time to time and stir.

Orange, Lime and Grand Marnier Ice Cream

Beechfield House, Beanacre
Chef/proprietor Peter Crawford-Rolt

Serves 8

8 egg yolks
11 oz. (300g.) castor sugar
1 pint (575ml.) milk
1 pint (575ml.) cream
3 fl.oz. (75ml.) Grand Marnier
½ teaspoon Orange Flower
  Water
zest 1 lime, blanched
zest 1 orange, blanched

Bring the milk and cream to the boil.

Whisk the sugar and egg yolks together and whisk into the just boiled milk and cream. Return to a gentle heat, stirring constantly, until the custard coats the back of a wooden spoon. Allow to cool.

When cool stir in the Grand Marnier, Orange Flower Water and lime zest to the custard. Place into ice cream machine or deep freeze. If using deep freeze, bring out from time to time and stir.

To serve, caramelise the orange zest. Top the ice cream with the orange zest and orange segments.

Parfait Praliné

Gasché's, Weybourne
Chef Nigel Massingham

Serves 8

1 lb. (450g.) cube sugar
¼ cup water
8 oz. (225g.) almonds, flaked
10 eggs
1 lb. (450g.) icing sugar
2 tablespoons castor sugar
1 pint (575ml.) double cream,
   whipped
2 measures Kirsch
2 measures Grand Marnier

Put the water and cube sugar in a saucepan and boil until the sugar is a golden brown. Take off heat and add the almonds. Allow to cool.

When cool, crush the almonds and sugar.

Separate the eggs. Put the yolks in a basin, add the icing sugar and whip over a saucepan of simmering water until fluffy. Transfer the mixture to a large basin.

Pour the whipped cream into the egg mixture. Whip 5 egg whites until stiff. Fold in the egg whites and castor sugar to the mixture. Add the Kirsch and Grand Marnier and stir. Fold in the crushed almonds and sugar. Turn into individual moulds and place into the deep freeze.

Petit Vacherin et sa Glace aux Pistils de Safran

Roux Restaurants Ltd
Albert and Michel Roux

Serves 6

18 fl.oz. (½ litre) milk
2 fl.oz. (50ml.) double cream
8 egg yolks
3½ oz. (100g.) castor sugar
1 soupspoon pure safran
6 round vacherin meringue
    bases
3 fresh peaches
red wine, for poaching the
    peaches

Using a wire whisk, work together the egg yolks and about one-third of the sugar in a bowl, until the whisk leaves a trail when lifted.

Put the milk in a saucepan with the remaining sugar and bring to the boil. Pour the boiling milk onto the egg mixture, whisking continuously. Pour back into the saucepan and set over low heat and cook. Stir continuously with a spatula, until the mixture is thick enough to coat it. Do not boil. Pass through a conical sieve and add the safran. Keep in a cool place until completely cold. Stir from time to time to prevent a skin from forming.

Put the mixture in a bowl and stir in the cream. Pour into an ice cream maker.

To serve, place the ice cream on each of the meringue bases. Place half a peach, which you have poached in the red wine, on top of the ice cream. Reduce the poaching liquid to a syrup and pour around.

This recipe will appear in the follow up to New Classic Cuisine, by Michel and Albert Roux (winner of 1984 Glenfiddick Award), Published by Macdonald & Co.

Pistachio Nut and Green Chartreuse Ice Cream

Partners 23, Sutton
Chef Andrew Thomason

Serves 6

6 egg yolks
4 oz. (125g.) castor sugar
5 tablespoons water
2 tablespoons icing sugar
Green Chartreuse to taste
6 oz. (175g.) pistachio nuts
green colouring
1 pint (575ml.) double cream

At Partners 23 we serve this ice cream in a Russe biscuit shell on a cold sabayon sauce, flavoured with Green Chartreuse. It is a soft ice cream and keeps well for several weeks.

Finely chop the pistachio nuts and save the dust. Pound the dust to a smooth paste with a little water and green colour to moisten.

Add this paste to the yolks and whisk until thick and an even pale green, about 5 minutes.

Meanwhile bring to the boil the sugar and the water. While still bubbling, trickle onto the yolks and whisk at a high speed until thickened and cold. Place in the freezer.

Whisk the cream, Chartreuse and icing sugar until thick. When the egg mixture starts to set, fold in the whipped cream and chopped pistachios. Freeze.

Poached Pears with Honey Ice Cream and Chocolate Sauce

The Ritz Hotel, London W1
Chef Michael Quinn

Serves 6

6 Comice or Conference pears,
  firm and large

For the syrup stock:
1 pint (575ml.) water
4 oz. (125ml.) castor sugar
1 pint (575ml.) water
4 oz. (125ml.) castor sugar
liqueurs, vanilla pod and cloves
  (optional)

For the ice cream:
1 pint (575ml.) milk
½ lb. (225g.) honey, flower
  based
8 egg yolks
1 pint (575 ml.) single cream

For the chocolate sauce:
½ pint (275ml.) double cream
½ lb. (225g.) plain chocolate
1 oz. (25g.) castor sugar
dark rum

Peel the pears, leaving the stalk intact, and poach gently in the syrup until cooked, while still keeping the flesh firm—about 4 minutes. Allow to cool in syrup.

Make the ice cream by boiling the milk. Mix together the honey and egg yolks and add to the milk. Allow to cool, add the cream and freeze.

Make the chocolate sauce by mixing all the ingredients together and bringing to the boil, whisking all the time. Pass through a fine strainer to remove any lumps.

Slice the top off the pears and part of the bottom so that there is an even base. Scoop out the pulp and fill with honey ice cream. Coat with 1 tablespoon of honey and pop the top back on. Coat with the hot chocolate sauce, leaving the stalks uncovered. Garnish with toasted almonds.

Praline Ice Cream

Sharrow Bay, Ullswater
Chef/proprietor Francis Coulson

Serves 8

1 pint (575ml.) double cream
1 pint (575ml.) milk
8 egg yolks
4 oz. (125g.) castor sugar
2 dessertspoons brandy

For the praline:

4 oz. (125g.) castor sugar
4 oz. (125g.) flaked almonds

Make the praline by putting the sugar and almonds into a heavy bottomed saucepan over heat. Leave to turn a caramel colour. Turn out onto a well oiled tin and leave to cool. Grind when required.

Bring the milk and cream to the boil. Whip the yolks and sugar together and whisk onto the milk. Return to a gentle heat and stir until the spatula is lightly coated. Do not boil. Stand in cold water to cool. When cool, fold in the rest of the cream.

Add the praline to the custard and mix well with brandy. Chill and freeze.

Prune and Armagnac Ice Cream

Hambleton Hall, Hambleton
Chef Nicholas Gill

Serves 8

8 oz. (225g.) prunes
5 fl.oz. (150ml.) water
5 fl.oz. (150ml.) red wine
rind 1 lemon
rind 1 orange
1 cinnamon stick
6 oz. (175g.) granulated sugar
squeeze lemon juice
½ pint (275ml.) double cream
1 tablespoon Armagnac or
 brandy

Place the prunes in a saucepan with the water, red wine, lemon rind, cinnamon stick and sugar. Cover and simmer for 45–60 minutes until tender. Drain well and reserve the juices.

Remove the stones from the prunes, then purée in a liquidiser or food processor until smooth. Transfer to a mixing bowl and blend in the Armagnac and the cooking juices. Taste and add a squeeze of lemon juice or a little sugar if needed.

Lightly whip the cream and fold in lightly to the mixture. Transfer to a plastic container and freeze until firm.

Raspberry Ice Cream

Box Tree, Ilkley
Chef Michael Lawson

12 oz. (350g.) fresh or frozen
  raspberries
6 oz. (175g.) castor sugar
15 fl.oz. (425ml.) double cream
juice 1 orange
juice 1 lemon
3 teaspoons iced water

Liquidise the raspberries and then pass through sieve to remove the seeds.

Mix the raspberry purée with the orange and lemon juice and the sugar. Chill this mixture in the refrigerator for 1 hour.

Whip the cream with the iced water until it forms soft peaks.

Mix the raspberry purée with the whipped cream and beat them lightly together. Place into ice cream machine or deep freeze.

Soufflé Glace aux Fraises

Le Gamin, London EC4
Chef Alban Reynaud

Serves 6

9 oz. (250g.) strawberry purée
5 egg whites
9 fl. oz. (250ml.) fresh cream, whipped
9 oz. (250g.) castor sugar
3 fl.oz. (75ml.) water
18 fl.oz. (500ml.) coulis of strawberries (passed through a sieve and sprinkled with sugar)

Bring the castor sugar and water to the boil. Stop cooking as soon as the temperature reaches 116° centigrade.

Whisk the egg whites until firm and fold in quickly to the syrup. Leave to cool and then add the strawberry purée and whipped cream.

Pour the mixture into individual moulds and pop into the freezer for 2 hours. Take out of moulds and pour coulis around.

65

Iced Soufflé with Poire William

Royal Crescent Hotel, Bath
Chef Raymond Duthie

Serves 6

5 whole eggs
8 oz. (225g.) castor sugar
½ pint (275ml.) double cream,
  partially whipped
2 good measures Poire William
  liqueur
cocoa powder

Whisk the eggs and sugar together, continually, over a pan of boiling water till stiff. Allow to cool until just warm.

Whip the cream with the Poire William.

Line a 6" soufflé mould, around the outside rim, with a 3" strip of greaseproof paper so that 2" protrudes above the rim. Bind with sellotape.

Gently fold the flavoured cream into the eggs and sugar and pour into the mould. Level the top and freeze.

To serve, remove the paper carefully. Draw a pear shape, with leaf attached, on the centre of a piece of stiff card. Using a carpet knife or something equally sharp, cut around the outline of the shape to leave a pear shaped hole. Hold this carefully on top of the soufflé and lightly dredge with cocoa powder through the hole to leave an attractive pear shaped design on the top of the soufflé. Serve immediately.

Strawberry and Passion Fruit Ice Cream

Partners 23, Sutton
Chef/proprietor Tim McEntire and partner, Andrew Thomason

Serves 8–10

For the custard:

6 egg yolks
5 oz. (150g.) sugar
1 pint (450ml.) milk

½ pint (275ml.) strawberry pulp
12 passion fruit
1½ pints (875ml.) whipping
  cream

Bring the milk to the boil.

Prepare the custard by whisking the yolks and sugar together over heat in a double boiler. After a minute they will have increased in volume, add the boiling milk and whisk well until it starts to thicken. Remove from heat and cool by whisking.

Mix half the custard with the strawberry pulp and the remainder with the juice and pips of the passion fruit. Leave to rest until cold. Pass each mixture through a fine sieve.

Lightly whip the cream and fold half with each mixture, keeping separate. Pour both mixtures together into your freezing container to obtain a marbled effect. Place into deep freeze.

To serve, place 2 well rounded scoops into a very large wine glass and garnish with a large strawberry cut into 4 lengthways keeping the green stalk intact. Arrange around the ice cream with a rosette of whipped cream and finish with a piped chocolate run out.

Tia Maria and Chocolate Ice Cream with Hazelnut Meringues

Riverside, Helford
Chef/proprietor George Perry-Smith

Serves 8

8 oz. (225g.) Menier chocolate
2 fl.oz. (50ml.) Tia Maria
2 large macaroons
½ pint (275ml.) double cream, whipped
1 dessertspoon Nescafé
4 egg whites, stiffly whipped

For the custard:

8 yolks
6 oz. (175g.) sugar
½ pint (275ml.) single cream

For the meringues:

2 egg whites
4 oz. (125g.) castor sugar
2 oz. (50g.) hazelnuts, chopped

Break up the macaroons and soak in the Tia Maria.

Bring the single cream just to the boil. Whisk the yolks and the sugar together and pour on the single cream. Transfer to a double boiler and cook, stirring all the time, until the custard coats the back of a spoon. Do not boil.

Melt the Nescafé and 3 oz. (75g.) of the chocolate in 2 fl.oz. (50ml.) of water. Add to the custard while still warm. Cool, then freeze. When almost solid, churn at top speed in a blender for 5 minutes with the whipped cream, the remaining 5 oz. (150g.) chocolate grated medium fine and the macaroons and Tia Maria. Add the whipped egg whites and churn again for 30 seconds. Re-freeze.

Serve with small hazelnut meringues and perhaps a very little more whipped cream.

Timbale Amelia

Billesley Manor, Stratford -upon-Avon
Chef Ian Whittock

For the Langues du Chat:

3½ oz. (110g.) butter
3½ oz. (110g.) castor sugar
3½ oz. (110g.) egg whites
3½ oz. (110g.) medium flour
vanilla flavouring

For the peach ice cream:

4 peaches, cooked
2 oz. (50g.) castor sugar
5 fl.oz. (150ml.) double cream
5 fl.oz. (150ml.) milk

8 large yellow peaches
fresh or tinned raspberries
Sauce Anglaise
poached apricots for garnish

Make the langues du chat, by blending all the ingredients together. Spoon the mix onto a buttered and floured tray, 1 spoon at a time. Bake in a hot oven until lightly browned. While still hot, mould the mix over 8 cups until cold.

Poach the 8 peaches and cut enough to remove the stone.

Make the ice cream by bringing the milk and cream just to the boil. Pulp the 4 peaches and add the sugar. Pour on the hot milk and cream and mix thoroughly until cold. Place in an ice cream machine or deep freeze.

To serve, fill each peach with the ice cream and place in the biscuit. Garnish with four halves of poached apricots and two rosettes of cream and chervil. For the sauce, pulp the raspberries and add sugar to taste and pour around the biscuit. Pipe three rings of the sauce Anglaise on and drag with a knife to make a pattern. You can, if you are feeling very keen, cover the basket with a similar shape of spun sugar to make a lid.

Toffee and Hazelnut Ice Cream

Fernie Lodge, Husbands Bosworth
Chef/proprietor Ishbel Speight

Serves 8

8 egg yolks
6 oz. (175g.) castor sugar
1½ pints (875ml.) milk
2 drops vanilla essence
1 lb. (450g.) granulated sugar
water
4 oz. (125g.) toasted
   hazelnuts, skinned and
   lightly crushed
¼ pint (150ml.) double cream,
   whipped

Put the granulated sugar into a pan with enough water to dissolve and keep liquid. Place onto heat and bring to the crack stage on your thermometer. Take off heat and add a little water.

Put the milk and vanilla essence onto the stove to warm.

Whisk the egg yolks and castor sugar in a bowl. When the milk is warm whisk into the egg mixture and return to the heat—do not boil—stirring continuously until the mixture coats the back of a spoon and leaves a mark when you run your finger over it.

Pour the hot mixture over the cooled sugar and mix well. Allow to go cold. When cold, place into ice cream machine or deep freeze. If using a deep freeze, stir every 10 minutes or so until partly frozen.

When the ice cream is partly frozen fold in the nuts and cream. Fold together twice more if using the deep freeze and then allow to completely set.

Vanilla, Hazelnut and Marsala Ice Cream

Hole in the Wall, Bath
Chef/proprietor Tim Cumming

Serves 8–10

8 egg yolks
8 oz. (225g.) vanilla sugar
1½ pints (875ml.) milk
2 drops vanilla essence
15 fl.oz. (425ml.) double cream
3 oz. (75g.) hazelnuts
2 fl.oz. (50ml.) Marsala

Lightly roast the hazelnuts and skin them.

Whisk the eggs and sugar together. Add the milk, which you have brought just to the boil, and the vanilla essence. Heat slowly but steadily, stirring all the time, till the mixture coats the back of a spoon. Sieve, whisk and set to cool.

When cool, add the cream and place in ice cream machine. When almost ready, add the roughly chopped hazelnuts and Marsala. Finish freezing.

Walnut Ice Cream

Gravetye Manor, East Grinstead
Chef Allan Garth

Serves 8

1¼ pints (750ml.) milk
11 oz. (300g.) castor sugar
12 egg yolks
pinch salt
11 oz. (300g.) double cream
5 oz. (150g.) marzipan
8 oz. (225g.) walnuts, ground

Whip the egg yolks and the sugar.

Bring the milk, salt and marzipan to the boil. Pour onto the egg mixture, stirring all the time.

Half whip the double cream. Stir in the cream and the walnuts to the mixture.

Place in an ice cream machine or the deep freeze. If using the deep freeze, bring out and stir from time to time.

Iced Whiskey Oranges

Ballymaloe House, Shanagarry
Chef/proprietor Myrtle Allen

6 oranges, halved
2 eggs
2 oz. (50g.) sugar
5 fl.oz. (150ml.) milk
½ pint (275ml.) whipped cream
1½ level teaspoons gelatin
2½ tablespoons Irish Whiskey

To decorate:

5 fl.oz. (150ml.) whipped cream
24 fresh bay leaves
2 tablespoons Irish Whiskey

Boil the sugar and milk together until thick. A drop falling from the side of a spoon should leave a slight thread.

Separate the yolks from the whites. Add the milk mixture gradually to the yolks. Beat to a thick mousse.

Squeeze the juice from the oranges and scrape the skins clean to leave nicely shaped orange halves.

Dissolve the gelatin in a little of the orange juice in a bowl over boiling water. Blend this carefully with 5 fl.oz. (150ml.) of the remaining juice. Cool.

Add the orange mixture and the whiskey to the yolks. Whip the egg whites stiffly and fold in. Fill into orange halves, heaping up as much as you can get in. Place in the deep freeze for 2 hours.

To serve, sweeten the whipped cream and add the whiskey. Pipe a line of the flavoured cream across the centre of each orange and place 2 bay leaves on either side.

This recipe appears in The Ballymaloe Cookbook by Myrtle Allen. Publishers Gill & McMillan, Dublin.

Sorbets

Apple Sultan Sorbet

Blostin's, Shepton Mallet
Chef/proprietor Monica Austin

For the ice cream:

1½ lb. (675g.) cooking apples
6 oz. (175g.) castor sugar
rind of 1 lemon
1″ cinnamon stick
1 pint (575ml.) water
juice 2 lemons
green colouring
2 fl.oz. (50ml.) brandy
5 fl.oz. (150ml.) cream,
  whipped

For the compôte:

8 oz. (225g.) sultanas
½ pint (275ml.) water
1 oz. (50g.) white rum
3 oz. (75g.) castor sugar
1 bay leaf
strip lemon peel

Peel and slice the apples. Put in a pan with the sugar, lemon peel, cinnamon and water. Bring to the boil and cook until the apples are tender. Add the lemon juice and colour slightly green. Put through a sieve, cool and add brandy.

Place into ice cream machine or deep freeze and leave until partly frozen. Add the whipped cream and finish freezing.

Make the compôte by simmering all the ingredients together until the mixture becomes like thick cream. Remove bay leaves and lemon peel and chill.

Serve the ice cream topped with the sultana compôte.

Apple and Calvados Sorbet

Fernie Lodge, Husbands Bosworth
Chef/proprietor Ishbel Speight

Serves 8

2 large Bramley apples
1 medium Cox's apple
1 pint (575ml.) dry cider
4 oz. (125g.) soft brown sugar
1 tablespoon double cream,
   beaten
2 tablespoons beaten egg
   whites
2 fl.oz. (50ml.) Calvados

Slice the apples, having removed the core but not the skin. Place into an ovenproof dish, sprinkle with the sugar and add dry cider. Cover with baking foil and place into preheated oven 350°F/180°C/gas 4. Cook apples until soft but not sloppy. Put to one side and allow to cool.

When cool either pass through a conical strainer or a liquidiser.

Place the mixture into an ice cream machine or deep freeze until partly frozen. Add the cream, egg white and Calvados and continue to freeze. If using the deep freeze, remove the sorbet from time to time and give a good stir. Serve with slices of apple to garnish.

Banana Sorbet

Billesley Manor, Stratford-upon-Avon
Chef Ian Whittock

Serves 8

2 pints (generous litre) water
8 oz. (225g.) sugar
2 lemons, cut in half
8 bananas, peeled
1 vanilla pod

Bring the water, sugar, lemons and vanilla pod to the boil.
Simmer for a few minutes and leave to cool.

Strain the syrup.

Put the banana flesh into a processor and whizz. Add to
the syrup and mix well together. You want a density of 22°
on the saccharometer.

Place into the ice cream machine or deep freeze. If using
the deep freeze, bring out from time to time and stir.

Blackberry Sorbet

Walnut Tree Inn, Llandewi Skirrid
Chef/proprietor Franco Taruschio

Serves 6

4 oz. (125g.) sugar
5 fl.oz. (125ml.) water
1 lb. (450g.) blackberries
2 tablespoons rosewater

Make a syrup by simmering the sugar and water for 5 minutes. Leave to cool.

Wash the blackberries and rub them through a sieve into a plastic container.

Add the syrup and rosewater to the blackberry purée.

Place in the ice cream machine or deep freeze. If using the deep freeze bring out after an hour and stir. When semi-frozen pass in an electric whisker until smooth and fluffy. Freeze.

Blackcurrant Leaf Sorbet

Arbutus Lodge, Cork
Chef/proprietor Declan Ryan

Serves 6

1 pint (575ml.) water
6 oz. (175g.) sugar
rind 2 lemons
juice 3 lemons
3 or 4 handfuls of blackcurrent
  leaves
little egg white, whipped

Make a mild lemon sorbet base by putting the lemon rind, juice, sugar and water in a pan. Bring to the boil.

Infuse the blackcurrant leaves in the hot sorbet mix.

Strain out the leaves when the flavour is strong enough.

Place into an ice cream machine or deep freeze. If using a deep freeze, bring out from time to time and stir.

The leaves discolour the mixture a bit, so add a little egg white to the sorbet to whiten when freezing.

79

Champagne Sorbet

Croque-en-Bouche, Malvern Wells
Chefs/proprietors Robin and Marion Jones

Serves 8

11 fl.oz. (300ml.) water
9 oz. (250g.) sugar
zest of lemon
½ bottle good full-flavoured
   Champagne e.g. Bollinger
juice 1 lemon
juice 1 small orange
2 egg whites
1 tablespoon sugar

Put the sugar and water in a pan over heat to dissolve the sugar and then bring to the boil to make a syrup. Steep the zest in the syrup until cool.

When cool, mix with the champagne and lemon and orange juice and place in ice cream machine or deep freeze. If using a deep freeze, bring out from time to time and stir.

As the sorbet solidifies, add the whites beaten stiff with the sugar. This sorbet is at its best when freshly made.

Pink Champagne Sorbet

Gravetye Manor, East Grinstead
Chef Allan Garth

Serves 12

½ bottle pink Champagne
9 fl.oz. (250ml.) stock syrup, at
  32° on the saccharometer
juice 1 lemon
9 fl.oz. (250ml.) fresh orange
  juice
3½ fl.oz. (100ml.) Curacao
3 pints (1½ litres) double
  cream

*This enriched sorbet is excellent when served with orange
or raspberries.*

Mix together all the above ingredients, except for the
cream. Place into an ice cream machine or deep freeze. If
using the deep freeze, remove from time to time and stir.

Half whip the cream.

When the sorbet is frozen, fold in the cream by hand. Pour
into a container and place in the freezer for about 4 hours
until frozen.

Damson Sorbet

Bistro Nine, Colchester
Chef/proprietor Penny Campbell

Serves 10

2 pints (generous litre) water
1 lb. (450g.) granulated sugar
2 lb. (900g.) fresh damsons
3 egg whites
sprigs fresh mint

Place the sugar and water in a heavy based saucepan and slowly bring to the boil. Boil gently for 10 minutes.

Add the damsons and cook until soft. Strain, retaining the sugar syrup. Rub the damsons through a sieve to give a thick purée. Add this purée to the syrup and cool.

Turn the mixture into a shallow tin and freeze until fairly solid. Whisk the egg whites until stiff and gradually spoon into the sorbet base, still mixing. Turn into containers and freeze, stirring occasionally.

Serve scooped into glass dishes and decorate with sprigs of fresh mint.

Elderflower Sorbet

French Partridge, Horton
Chef/proprietor David Partridge

18 heads of elderflower,
   washed
1½ lb. (675g.) castor sugar
1½ pints (875ml.) water
1 oz. (25g.) tartaric acid
½ lemon, sliced
2 oranges, sliced
1 egg white

Place everything into a large container and stir from time to time, over a minimum period of 24 hours. Strain the liquid.

This liquid will be of cordial strength and may need diluting with water—you need to achieve a reading of 15° sugar strength on the saccharometer.

Place into an ice cream machine or deep freeze. Towards the end of the freezing process, whisk in one egg white to improve the texture. Return to freezer.

Exotic Sorbet

Manley's, Storrington
Chef/proprietor Karl Löderer

Purée of the following:

3 large ripe mangoes
3 paw-paw
3 guavas
½ medium sized pineapple
2 bananas

juice 2 lemons
juice 1 lime
15 fl.oz. (425ml.) fresh orange
  juice
1 small egg white, whipped
grated fresh nutmeg, to taste
1 measure dark rum, to taste
1 measure Cointreau, to taste
1 measure Curacao, to taste

Make 5 fl.oz. (150ml.) of sugar syrup by mixing together 6 fl.oz. (175ml.) water, 3 oz. (75g.) sugar and ¼ oz. (7g.) glucose. Bring to the boil and simmer for 10 minutes. Allow to cool.

Mix the sugar syrup together with all the other ingredients and transfer to ice cream machine.

Gewurztraminer Sorbet

Priory Hotel, Bath
Chef Mike Collom

Serves 8

1 lb. (450g.) granulated sugar
1 pint (575ml.) water
½ bottle Gewurztraminer
juice 1 orange
juice 1 lemon
3 egg whites

Because of its high alcohol content this sorbet will never set very hard and it makes a delightful start or finish to any meal. One of my favourites is to place a scoop in half an Ogen melon, decorated with black and white grapes.

Bring the sugar and water to the boil and simmer for 10 minutes. Set aside to cool.

Pour the wine and an equal amount of sugar syrup as well as the lemon and orange juice into a bowl and mix well.

Place into an ice cream machine or deep freeze. If you are using the deep freeze, take out from time to time and stir: add 3 lightly beaten egg whites, which will act as a stabiliser and will prevent your sorbet from separating.

Gin and Tonic Sorbet

Hambleton Hall, Hambleton
Chef Nicholas Gill

1 wine glass (7 fl.oz.–200ml.)
  gin
2 wine glasses (7 fl.oz.–200ml.)
  tonic
juice 3 lemons
teaspoon egg white
½ pint (275ml.) stock syrup
juniper berries, for decoration
sprigs of mint, for decoration

Make a stock syrup. You want to achieve 24° on the saccharometer.

Mix the cooled syrup with the gin, tonic and lemon juice. Place into ice cream machine or deep freeze. If using the deep freeze, bring out from time to time and stir. When partly frozen add the egg white and complete freezing process.

To serve, pipe the sorbet into frosted glasses. Decorate with a juniper berry and a sprig of mint.

Ginger Water Ice

Horn of Plenty, Gulworthy
Chef/proprietor Sonia Stevenson

Serves 8

13 oz. (375g.) sugar
1 pint (575ml.) water
4 lemons
8 grapefruit
3 large tablespoons stem
    ginger, puréed (to taste)

In a pan, boil together the sugar, water and zest of the lemon and grapefruit, which you have removed with a potato peeler. Cool.

Squeeze the juice from the fruit and add to the sugar mixture. Cool and chill till just frozen.

When just frozen whisk in a liquidiser with the puréed stem ginger. Re-freeze till very firm.

Gooseberry and Apple Mint Sorbet

Cromlix House, Dunblane
Chef Mark Napper

Serves 8

For the syrup:

2¼ lb. (1 kilo) granulated or
    castor sugar
2½ pints (1¼ litres) water
7 oz. (175g.) glucose

2 lb. (900g.) fresh gooseberries
1 oz. (50g.) sugar
3 sprigs fresh apple mint, finely
    chopped

Combine all the ingredients for the syrup in a heavy based pan and set over a high heat, stirring occasionally with a wooden spatula. Bring the mixture to the boil and leave to bubble for several minutes, skimming the surface if necessary.

Pass through a conical sieve into a bowl and allow to cool.

Simmer the gooseberries, sugar and 2 tablespoons of water till soft. Pass through a medium to fine sieve. Add the finely chopped apple mint, cool and mix with 1 pint (575ml.) of the sorbet syrup.

Place into ice cream machine or deep freeze. If using a deep freeze, take out from time to time and stir.

Gooseberry Water Ice

Plough Inn, Fadmoor
Chef/proprietor Kath Brown

1 lb. (450g.) green
   gooseberries
8 oz. (225g.) castor sugar
1 pint (575ml.) water
2 large lemons
green food colouring

This is a very useful recipe as it is sharp enough to refresh the palate between savoury courses, but is fruity enough to serve as a dessert. Very good with a rich vanilla or lemon ice cream.

There is no need to top and tail the gooseberries.

Simmer with sugar and water until they begin to burst. Sieve.

Add the juice of the lemons and a very little food colouring. Cool and place into ice cream machine or deep freeze. If using deep freeze, bring out from time to time and beat well.

Grapefruit Sorbet

Sharrow Bay, Ullswater
Chef/proprietor Francis Coulson

Serves 8

1 pint (575ml.) water
12 oz. (350g.) granulated sugar
4 grapefruit

Bring the sugar and water to the boil in a pan.

Remove the rind from the grapefruits and squeeze out all the juice.

Add the grapefruit juice to the syrup and boil for 10 minutes.

Leave this syrup to marinate overnight and then strain through a sieve. Place into an ice cream machine or into the deep freeze. If using a deep freeze, remove the mixture from time to time and stir.

Grapefruit and Campari Sorbet

Homewood Park, Hinton Charterhouse
Chef/proprietor Stephen Ross

1 pint (575ml.) water
8 oz. (225g.) sugar
7 fl.oz. (200ml.) wine glass
   Campari
1 pint (575ml.) fresh grapefuit
juice

Make a syrup from the water and sugar by bringing to the boil and cooking until the sugar has dissolved. Allow to cool.

Mix the cold syrup with the rest of the ingredients and place into an ice cream machine or the deep freeze. If using the deep freeze, remove and stir as often as possible before it sets.

Sorbet de Pamplemousse Rose et Gin

Restaurant Bosquet, Kenilworth
Chef/proprietor Bernard Lignier

Serves 8

18 fl.oz. (500ml.) pink
   grapefruit juice
5 fl.oz. (150ml.) water
3½ fl.oz. (100ml.) gin
5 oz. (150g.) sugar

This delicious sorbet is very good when served as a first course in the summer months.

Bring the water and sugar to the boil, and cook for 3 minutes. Allow to cool. When cold add the grapefruit juice and gin.

Place into an ice cream machine or deep freeze. If using a deep freeze, remove from time to time and stir.

Sorbet à la Guinness

Marlfield House, Gorey
Chef/proprietor Mary Bowe

Serves 12

1 lb. (450g.) sugar
2 pints (generous litre) water
1 pint of Guinness
water to taste

Make a syrup by dissolving the sugar in the water. You want to reach 15° on the saccharometer. Allow to cool.

Add the Guinness to the syrup and taste. The syrup should not overcome the bitterness of the Guinness.

Place into an ice cream machine or deep freeze. If using a deep freeze, bring out from time to time and stir well.

Kiwi Fruit Sorbet

No 3, Glastonbury
Chef/proprietor Jillian Gilliat

Serves 8

1 lb. (450g.) granulated sugar
1½ pints (875ml.) water
4 kiwi fruit
zest and juice 4 lemons
green vegetable colouring
2 egg whites, lightly beaten

Make a syrup by heating together gently in a heavy pan the sugar and water. Boil fast for 4 minutes and allow to cool.

Peel and liquidise the kiwi fruit along with the zest and juice of the lemons. Add the sugar syrup and freeze.

When softly frozen, incorporate the lightly beaten egg whites and green colouring for the desired effect. Finish freezing.

Lemon and Pernod Sorbet

Paul's, Folkestone
Chef/proprietor Paul Hagger

Serves 10

3 measures Pernod
12 lemons
5 oz. (150g.) sugar
1 pint (575ml.) water
12 egg whites

Peel and grate the rind from the lemons. Boil the peel till soft in the water and sugar.

Strain off the peel and set aside.

Juice the lemons and add to the sugar mixture.

Freeze till soft snow consistency. If using deep freeze, give a vigorous stir about 4 times during freezing process.

Beat egg whites till stiff but not grainy and add the Pernod. Mix with the sorbet. Re-freeze and if using deep freeze whisk twice more.

When set but still a little soft, beat the remaining egg whites till stiff and gently fold both together, adding the peel at the same time.

Remove from freezer 10 minutes before serving and decorate with a little of the peel and a little biscuit.

Lime Sorbet

Royal Crescent Hotel, Bath
Chef Raymond Duthie

Serves 8

2 lb. (generous kilo) sugar
1¾ pints (litre) water
juice 1 lemon
finely grated zest and juice of
    4 limes
1 egg white

Mix the sugar and water together and slowly bring to the boil, carefully removing the scum from the surface as it appears. Boil for 2–3 minutes and then allow to cool.

Add the lemon juice, lime juice, zest and the egg white and mix well. Place into ice cream machine or deep freeze. If using the deep freeze, take out from time to time and stir.

Mango Sorbet

Hole in the Wall, Bath
Chef/proprietor Tim Cumming

Serves 6

1 Golden Delicious apple
3–4 ripe mangoes
juice ½ lemon
5 oz. (150g.) sugar
2 fl.oz. (50ml.) double cream
1 egg white

Peel and core and quarter the apple.

Peel, de-stone and chunk the mangoes. Liquidise the apple and mango flesh in a processor with the sugar and lemon juice. Leave for 1 minute and add the cream and egg white. Process for a further minute.

Place the mixture in an ice cream machine or deep freeze. If using a deep freeze, take out from time to time and stir.

Sorbet Marc de Bourgogne

Gidleigh Park, Chagford
Chef/proprietor Kay Henderson

Serves 8

2 pints (generous litre) water
15 oz. (425g.) sugar
juice 2 or 3 lemons
4 fl.oz. (125ml.) Marc de
  Bourgogne

Bring the sugar and water to the boil. Heat until the sugar has dissolved. Allow to cool and pop into refrigerator.

When ready to freeze add the lemon juice. Put into ice cream machine or deep freeze.

When half frozen add the Marc de Bourgogne and finish freezing, stirring occasionally if using the deep freeze.

Melon and Ginger Sorbet

Box Tree, Ilkley
Chef Michael Lawson

Serves 8

5 oz. (150g.) sugar
1 lb. (450g.) melon flesh
8 oz. (225g.) stem ginger,
   chopped

In this beautifully refreshing sorbet, the melon purée and the sugar act as the basic sorbet mix.

Blend the melon to a purée and chill.

When cold, combine the rest of the ingredients together and add to the melon. Place into ice cream machine or deep freeze. If using a deep freeze, take out from time to time and stir.

Mint and Grapefruit Sorbet

Ston Easton Park, Ston Easton
Chef Robert Jones

Serves 8–10

1½ lb. (675g.) granulated sugar
3 pints (1½ litres) water
2 oranges, halved
1 lemon, halved
1 cinnamon stick
2 bay leaves
3 sprigs fresh mint (or a few
   drops mint essence)
juice 2 grapefruits
3 egg whites

Bring the sugar, water, oranges, lemon, cinnamon, bay leaves and the mint to the boil and cook for 15–20 minutes. Cool.

When cool, pass through a fine sieve into a clean container.

Add the grapefruit juice and some finely diced mint leaves. Take approximately ⅓ of the syrup and put into ice cream machine. Just as this is setting whip one egg white and fold into sorbet. Complete process and place into plastic container in deep freeze. Repeat this process twice more, adding the sorbet to the container in the deep freeze.

If no ice cream machine is available, place into deep freeze and stir every 10 minutes until it begins to set—add whipped egg whites and leave to set.

Mint Tea Sorbet

Walnut Tree Inn, Llandewi Skirrid
Chef/proprietor Franco Taruschio

Serves 6

12 oz. (350g.) sugar
1¾ pints (1 litre) water
⅓ oz. (10g.) tea
2 oz. (50g.) mint leaves

Put the sugar and water in a pan and bring to the boil for 1 minute.

Infuse the tea in the syrup for ½ minute. Strain. Then immerse the mint leaves in the infusion and allow to go cold.

Drain and squeeze the mint leaves till all the liquid is out. Place into ice cream machine or deep freeze and leave until half frozen. Then remove and pass in an electric mixer until fluffy. Re-freeze.

Granité of Muscat de Beaumes de Venise

Partners 23, Sutton
Chef/proprietor Tim McEntire and partner, Andrew Thomason

Serves 10

7 fl.oz. (200ml.) water
7 oz. (200g.) sugar
1 x 750ml. bottle Muscat de
    Beaumes de Venise
juice 1 orange
juice 1 lemon
small mint leaves for garnish

Boil the water and sugar together for 1 minute. Pour into a bowl and allow to cool.

When the syrup is cold, add the wine, orange and lemon juice and mix well together.

Pour into a large shallow tray and place in the freezer. During the course of the day lightly fork through the mixture to form small flakes.

Serve by filling long stem glasses with granité and garnish with a leaf of mint.

Orange and Campari Sorbet

Manley's, Storrington
Chef/proprietor Karl Löderer

12½ fl.oz. (360ml.) water
6 oz. (175g.) sugar
½ oz. (15g.) glucose
juice 10 medium sized
    oranges
juice 1 lemon
juice 1 lime
½ egg white
2 large measures Campari

Make a syrup by putting the water, sugar and glucose in a pan and bring to the boil. Simmer for 15 minutes.

Mix the syrup together with the rest of the ingredients, except the egg white, and transfer to ice cream machine.

When the sorbet has almost finished freezing, add the egg white. Finish freezing.

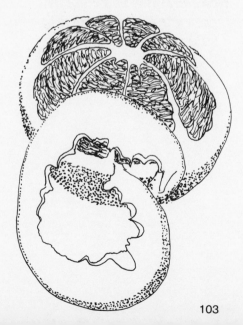

Passion Fruit and Lime Sorbet

Blostin's, Shepton Mallet
Chef/proprietor Bill Austin

Serves 8

8 oz. (225g.) castor sugar
1 pint (575ml.) water
4 limes
6 cooking apples, peeled and cored
4 egg whites
1 pint (575ml.) passion fruit pulp (about 32), reserving a little for decoration

Boil the sugar, water and rinds of limes for 10 minutes. Strain and cool.

Cook the apples in lime juice. Liquidise and cool. Add the apple and lime purée to the syrup. Add the passion fruit pulp and place in the freezer. When it begins to set, whisk the egg whites and fold in. Freeze until set.

15 minutes before serving, transfer to a refrigerator to soften slightly.

Decorate with strained passion fruit juice poured over.

Paw-Paw Sorbet

Bodysgallen Hall, Llandudno
Chef David Harding

Serves 8

2 lb., 14 oz. (1½ kilos) paw-paw
  fruit
7 oz. (200g.) castor sugar
1 tablespoon Kirsch
juice 1 lemon
1 egg white

Purée the fruit in a blender.

Add the lemon juice and sugar to the fruit purée.

Whisk the white of egg and fold into the mixture. Add the Kirsch.

Place into ice cream machine or deep freeze. If using the deep freeze, bring out from time to time and stir.

Pear Sorbet with Liqueur

Hole in the Wall, Bath
Chef/proprietor Tim Cumming

Serves 6–8

1½ lb. (675g.) pears (Williams),
 peeled
2 pints (generous litre) water
1 lb. (450g.) sugar
juice ½ lemon
1 egg white
2 fl.oz. (50ml.) Poire William
 liqueur

In a heavy pan, bring the sugar and water to the boil to make a syrup.

Poach the pears in the syrup until tender. Set aside to cool. Drain the pears, quarter and core. Liquidise in a food processor, adding ½ pint (275ml.) of the poaching syrup, the lemon juice and the egg white. Add the liqueur near the end.

Place into ice cream machine or deep freeze. If using the deep freeze, take out from time to time and stir.

When serving pour over an extra tot of the pear liqueur.

Pear and Quince Sorbet

The Market, Manchester
Chef/proprietor Lin Scrannage

1 lb. (450g.) William or
  Conference Pears (ripe)
8 oz. (225g.) quince
4 oz. (125g.) unsalted butter
small piece cinnamon stick
sugar to taste (4 oz.–125g. or
  more)
2 egg whites
toasted almonds, chopped

I was fortunate enough to have a couple of pounds of quinces given to me, so was able to make a delicious ice cream version of the sorbet as well:– the sorbet, however, is definitely the best—a most unusual and fruity flavour.

Wash and cut up the whole fruit, removing the stalks. Put in a pan with the butter, 2 fl.oz. (50ml.) water and the cinnamon. Stew slowly, covered, until tender. Purée in a liquidiser and put through a sieve to remove any pips. Add sugar to taste and make up to 2 pints (generous litre) with water. Cool.

Put into ice cream machine or deep freeze. If using a deep freeze, pour into a plastic container. When mushy beat the egg whites till stiff and mix into sorbet. Beat the sorbet twice at hourly intervals if using deep freeze.

This makes a soft textured sorbet, so just 30 minutes in the refrigerator will be enough to soften. Serve with a sprinkle of toasted chopped almonds.

Pineapple and Grenadine Sorbet

The Peat Inn, Peat Inn, Fife
Chef/proprietor David Wilson

Serves 6

1 lb. 4 oz. (575g.) ripe
   pineapple flesh
1½ sherry glasses Grenadine
3 oz. (75g.) icing sugar
1 dessertspoon liquid glucose

Slice both ends off the pineapple. Peel the pineapple, removing any black spots from the flesh. Slice into thick rings and core.

You require 1 lb. 4 oz. (575g.) of flesh, so weigh it to check. Chop and put into liquidiser or food processor. Add the Grenadine, icing sugar and liquid glucose. Liquidise again.

Strain the mixture through a conical strainer. Place into ice cream machine or deep freeze. If using the deep freeze, take out from time to time and stir.

Plum Sorbet

French Partridge, Horton
Chef/proprietor David Partridge

Serves 8

2 lb. (900g.) plums (we use
   Czars for a rich coloured
   juice)
1 lb. (450g.) castor sugar
water as required
1 egg white

Put the plums into a saucepan and just cover with water. Simmer until the stones can be easily removed. Add the sugar and stir in well. When the sugar has dissolved liquidise or pass through a sieve.

Using a saccharometer, check for the density of sugar—a reading of 15° is required—and dilute with water if necessary.

Place into an ice cream machine or deep freeze. Towards the end of the freezing process add the whipped egg white, which will result in an improved texture. Return to freezer.

Plum and Vodka Sorbet

Longueville Manor, Jersey
Chef John Dicken

1 lb. (450g.) Santa Rosa plums
8 oz. (225g.) sugar
½ pint (275ml.) water
5 fl.oz. (150ml.) white wine
3 measures vodka
juice ½ lemon

Mix the water, white wine, sugar and lemon juice together. Bring to the boil.

Meanwhile prepare the plums by removing the stones.

Cook the plums in the stock syrup for 5 minutes. Put into a liquidiser and blend until smooth. Pass through a chinoise or sieve.

Add the vodka and place into ice cream machine or deep freeze. If using a deep freeze, bring out from time to time and stir.

Pomegranate Sorbet

Carved Angel, Dartmouth
Chef/proprietor Joyce Molyneaux

Serves 6–8

15 fl.oz. (425ml.) pomegranate
   juice (6–8 fruit)
8 oz. (225g.) sugar
½ pint (275ml.) water
juice ½ lemon
2 fl.oz. (50ml.)

Make a syrup by putting the sugar in a pan with the water and bringing to the boil. Allow to cool.

Add the rest of the ingredients to the cold syrup.

Place into an ice cream machine or deep freeze. If using a deep freeze, bring out from time to time and stir well.

Quince and Mint Sorbet

Beechfield House, Beanacre
Chef/proprietor Peter Crawford-Rolt

Serves 8

For the stock syrup:

22 fl.oz. (625ml.) water
20 oz. (575g.) castor sugar

1 lb. (450g.) quinces, not
   peeled but quartered
8 oz. (225g.) granulated sugar
1 pint (575ml.) water
juice 4 lemons
small bunch fresh mint, finely
   shredded
fresh mint to garnish
wedges lime to garnish

Make a syrup with the water and castor sugar by dissolving the sugar and bringing to the boil. Simmer fast for 5 minutes.

Bring the quinces, granulated sugar and water to the boil and simmer until quinces are cooked. Pass the pulp of the quinces through a fine sieve. To the pulp, add the lemon juice and the finely shredded mint.

Combine the sorbet syrup and the quince pulp and place in ice cream machine or deep freeze. If using a deep freeze, bring out from time to time and stir. Serve with a sprig of fresh mint and a small wedge of lime.

Sorbet de Raisin

Mallory Court, Bishops Tachbrook
Chef Allan Holland

Serves 6

1 lb. (450g.) purple or red
   grapes
8 oz. (225g.) granulated sugar
½ pint (275ml.) water
2 good fl.oz. (50ml.) lemon
   juice

In a food processor or liquidiser, purée the grapes.

Strain purée through a fine sieve. Set over a bowl and press on the purée to extract all the juice. Reserve solids that are left and chill the juice.

In a small saucepan put the reserved solids together with the sugar and water and bring to the boil stirring occasionally and allow mixture to simmer for 5 minutes. Strain the resulting syrup through a fine sieve into a bowl and discard the solids.

When the syrup is cold, chill for an hour or so. Add the reserved grape juice to the syrup and lemon juice and freeze. If using deep freeze, bring out from time to time and stir.

Raspberry Sorbet

The Old Monastery, Drybridge
Chef/proprietor Douglas Craig

2 lb. (scant kilo) raspberries
8 oz. (225g.) redcurrants
juice 1 large lemon
juice 1 large orange
8 oz. (225g.) granulated sugar
5 fl.oz. (150ml.) water

This quantity will fill a 4 lb. (2 kilo) plastic container, which should be washed and sterilized and placed in the freezer to cool.

Dissolve the sugar in the water and boil for 3–4 minutes.

Heat the redcurrants gently until the juices run out. Squash with a wooden spoon. Remove from heat and add the orange and lemon juice.

Purée the raspberries in a blender and then push through a wire sieve, using a soup ladle, followed by the redcurrants with all the juices. Add the syrup and chill thoroughly, preferably overnight.

Place the mixture into a large shallow container, preferably metal, and place in deep freeze. Whisk at least 3 times while freezing. When nearly frozen, pack into the plastic container and seal.

Rose Petal Sorbet

Pool Court, Pool-In-Wharfdale
Chef Melvyn Jordan

6 oz. (175g.) granulated sugar
15 fl.oz. (425ml.) water
juice 1 small lime
4 oz. (125g.) rose petals
Rose Pink Colour as desired
rosewater to taste
2 egg whites, lightly beaten

This dish is unusual but quite delicious and should really be made in summer or autumn when rose petals are abundant. At Pool Court I religiously send the gardener out once a week to collect the drooping heads and make them into a syrup which freezes well, until we have enough without having stripped the garden. Make sure your roses have not been treated with pesticides!

Make a stock syrup with the sugar and water, stirring well. Add lime juice and bring to the boil and simmer for about 10 minutes. Pour over washed rose petals and leave to get cold. Liquidise and pass through coarse strainer. Add a few drops of rose water and rose colour.

Place into ice cream machine for about 20 minutes and then add the egg whites gradually to the sorbet. If you do not have an ice cream machine place into a plastic container with a lid and pop into deep freeze. Stir every 15 minutes or so until set. Then fold in egg whites as above.

Soupe au Fraises

La Potinière, Gullane
Chef/proprietor Hilary Brown

Serves 8

1¼ lb. (575g.) strawberries
3 oz. (75g.) castor sugar
juice ½ lemon
juice ½ orange
1 tablespoon Kirsch or
   Framboise Eau de Vie

For the custard:

3 egg yolks
2½ oz. (60g.) castor sugar
½ pint (275ml.) milk

Purée 8 oz. (225g.) of the strawberries. Add the sugar and the fruit juices. Sieve into a container and freeze.

Make a custard by heating the milk to just boiling. Whisk the egg yolks and sugar together. Add the milk, beating all the time. Return to a gentle heat and, beating constantly, cook till the custard coats the back of a spoon. Do not boil. Allow to cool and add the Kirsch or Framboise.

To serve, cover the base of 4 large, flat plates with the custard. Arrange halved strawberries, cut side down, attractively over the custard, leaving a space in the centre. Remove the frozen strawberry purée from the freezer, cut into pieces and blend in food processor till smooth. Then very quickly spoon the sorbet into the centre of each plate. Decorate with leaves of fresh mint and serve immediately.

116

Strawberry Sherbert

Sharrow Bay, Ullswater
Chef/proprietor Francis Coulson

1½ lb. (675g.) strawberries
4 oranges
1½ lemons
1 lb. (450g.) castor sugar
15 fl.oz. (425ml.) port
15 fl.oz. (425ml.) semi-sweet
   wine
dash of Kirsch

For the syrup:

14 oz. (400g.) castor sugar
1¾ pints (litre) water

Make a syrup by dissolving the sugar in the water and boiling.

Hull the strawberries and liquidise with rind from the oranges and lemons.

Segment the fruit and liquidise. Then pass all the ingredients through a sieve. Mix with the port and wine and Kirsch. Stir in the sugar and place into an ice cream machine or deep freeze. If using a deep freeze, bring out from time to time and stir.

Strawberry Water Ice

Ballymaloe House, Shanagarry
Chef/proprietor Myrtle Allen

Serves 8

2 lb. (900g.) strawberries
1 lb. (450g.) sugar
¾ pint (425ml.) water
juice 1 small lemon
2 egg whites
icing sugar

Hull and mash the strawberries with a fork, or alternatively spin in a liquidiser until they are in small pieces stopping just before the purée stage.

Boil the sugar and water steadily for about 2 minutes. Cool and add to the fruit, with the juice of the lemon, tasting as you go to ensure that the purée mixture is not too sweet. Stir well and freeze.

When almost set, whip the egg whites very stiffly. Add icing sugar and beat again. Take the strawberry mixture from the freezer and beat well in a chilled bowl to break up the ice crystals, stopping before it melts. Fold in the egg whites and refreeze.

This recipe appears in the Ballymaloe Cookbook by Myrtle Allen. Publishers Gill & McMillan, Dublin.

Tomato Sorbet with Fennel

Fernie Lodge, Husbands Bosworth
Chef/proprietor Ishbel Speight

Serves 8

2½ lb. (generous kilo)
  tomatoes
½ pint (275ml.) double cream,
  stiffly whisked
4 oz. (125g.) prawns, coarsely
  chopped
1 tablespoon tomato purée
½ teaspoon sugar
1 teaspoon fennel fern,
  chopped
1 teaspoon anchovy essence
dash Worcester sauce

This recipe makes an interesting and unusual starter for the summer months.

Skin the tomatoes and remove the seeds. Liquidise the flesh.

Mix together the tomato pulp, tomato purée, sugar, anchovy essence and fennel fern. Season with salt and black pepper. Fold in the cream and prawns and re-season to taste.

Place the mixture into small moulds and freeze for 3–4 hours.

The sorbet should be served half frozen, so turn onto plates a few minutes before serving. Garnish each portion with a wedge of lemon and whole prawns.

Notes

Notes

Drybridge

Peat Inn
Dunblane
Gullane

Ullswater

Fadmore
Ilkley
Pool in Wharfdale

Kenilworth

Dublin   Manchester   Husbands Bosworth

Llandudno   Weybourne

Gorey   Hambleton
                                                     Bishops Tachbrook
Shanagarry   Bishop' Cleeve   Horton
Cork   Malvern Wells   Stratford-on-Avon
                         Ledbury   Colchester
                Llandewi Skirrid Wye   Bray
                                    Stow on the Wold London
                          Painswick
                          Bristol   East Grinstead
Bath   Folkestone
                 Farrington Gurney
Ston Easton   Storrington
Glastonbury
                 Chagford
                                  Shepton Mallet   Beanacre
                      Dartmouth   Hinton Charterhouse
Jersey   Sark   Gulworthy   Warminster
              Helford

122

Restaurant Addresses

Arbutus Lodge	– St. Luke's Cross, Montenotte, Cork.	Cork 501237
Aval du Creux	– Harbour Hill, Sark, Channels Islands.	(0481 83) 2036
Ballymaloe House	– Shanagarry, Co. Cork.	Cork 652531
Beechfield House	– Beanacre, Melksham.	(0225) 703700
Billesley Manor	– Billesley, Nr. Stratford-upon-Avon.	(0789) 763737
Bistro Nine	– 9 North Hill, Colchester.	(0206) 576466
Blostin's	– Shepton Mallet, Somerset.	(0749) 3648
Bodysgallen Hall	– Llandudno, Gwynedd.	(0492) 84466
Restaurant Bosquet	– 97a Warwick Road, Kenilworth.	(0926) 52463
Box Tree	– Church Street, Ilkley.	(0943) 608484
Carved Angel	– 2 South Embankment, Dartmouth.	(08043) 2465
Chez Moi	– 3 Addison Avenue, London W11.	01 603 8267
Chez Nico	– 129 Queenstown Road, London SW8.	01 720 6960
Cleeveway House	– Evesham Road, Bishops Cleeve.	(024267) 2585
Coopers	– 28 High Street, Warminster.	(0985) 216911
Le Coq Hardi	– 35 Pembroke Road, Dublin.	Dublin 689070
Country Elephant	– Painswick, Glos.	(0452) 813564
Cromlix House	– Dunblane, Perthshire.	(0786) 822125
Croque-en-Bouche	– 221 Wells Road, Malvern Wells.	(06845) 65612
Fernie Lodge	– Berridge Lane, Husbands Bosworth.	(0858) 880551
French Partridge	– Horton, Nr. Northampton.	(0604) 870033
Le Gamin	– 32 Old Bailey, London EC4.	01 236 7931
Gashcé's	– Weybourne, Norfolk.	(026 370) 220
Gidleigh Park	– Chagford, Devon.	(064 73) 2311
Gravetye Manor	– Sharpthorne, Nr. East Grinstead.	(0342) 810567
Hambleton Hall	– Hambleton, Oakham.	(0572) 56991
Hole in the Wall	– 16 George Street, Bath.	(0225) 25242
Homewood Park	– Hinton Charterhouse, Bath.	(022 122) 2643
Hope End	– Ledbury, Hereford and Worcester.	(0531) 3613
Horn of Plenty	– Gulworthy, Nr. Tavistock.	(0822) 832528

Lichfield's	– 13 Lichfield Terrace, Richmond.	01 940 5236
Longueville Manor	– Jersey, Channel Islands.	(0534) 25501
Mallory Court	– Bishops Tachbrook, Nr. Leamington Spa.	(0926) 30214
Manley's	– Manley's Hill, Storrington.	(09066) 2331
The Market	– 30 Edge Street, Manchester.	(061 834) 3743
Marlfield House	– Gorey, Co. Wexford.	Gorey 21124
Mijanou	– 143 Ebury Street, London SW1.	01 730 4099
No. 3	– Magdalene Street, Glastonbury.	(0458) 32129
Old Monastery	– Drybridge, Banffshire.	(0542) 32660
Old Parsonage	– Farrington Gurney, Avon.	(0761) 52211
Partners 23	– 23 Stonecot Hill, Sutton.	01 644 7743
Paul's	– 2a Bouverie Road West, Folkestone.	(0303) 59697
The Peat Inn	– Peat Inn, Fife.	(033 484) 206
Plough Inn	– Fadmoor, North Yorkshire.	(0751) 31515
Pomegranates	– 94 Grosvenor Road, London SW1.	01 644 7743
Pool Court	– Pool in Wharfedale, West Yorkshire.	(0532) 842288
La Potinière	– Gullane, East Lothian.	(0620) 843214
The Priory	– Weston Road, Bath.	(0225) 331922
Rafters	– Park Street, Stow on the Wold.	(0451) 30200
The Ritz	– Piccadilly, London W1.	01 493 8181
Riverside	– Helford, Cornwall.	(032 623) 443
Royal Crescent Hotel	– Royal Crescent, Bath.	(0225) 319090
Sharrow Bay	– Honiton Road, Ullswater.	(085 36) 301
Ston Easton Park	– Ston Easton, Somerset.	(076 121) 631
Walnut Tree	– Llandewi Skirrid, Gwent.	(0873) 2797
Waterside Inn	– Ferry Road, Bray.	(0628) 20691
Wife of Bath	– 4 Upper Bridge Street, Wye.	(0233) 812540

Index

Cookery books from
Absolute Press

The Restaurant Recipe Book—£2.95

The first of the cookery books featuring recipes from West Country Restaurants.

**'How the editor has persuaded such notables as these to give up the secrets
which have made their establishments so exclusive is beyond my
comprehension.'**
Ray Tennyson, Somerset & West Monthly.

**'The Restaurant Recipe Book is strictly for best. It is the sort of tome you reach for
when entertaining and want to impress with a menu of gourmet dimensions.'**
Sally Rowat, Glos. and Avon Life.

' . . . a lasting souvenir to experiment with West Country cooking.'
Gail Duff.

The 2nd Restaurant Recipe Book—£2.95

Prompted by the tremendous success of the first book, this second collection of
recipes provides further mouthwatering recipes from the leading restaurants in
the West Country.

The London Restaurant Recipe Book—£3.95

The third book in this very popular series of recipes from leading English restaurants.
Featuring recipes from the capital city, with contributing restaurants of the calibre
of La Tante Claire, Chez Nico, The Ritz, Carriers, Lichfields and Boulestin.
Filled with fabulous recipes from fabulous restaurants.

Vegetarian Cuisine—£5.95

The perfect solution to that age old problem of what to cook when vegetarian friends come to dinner. A refreshingly original collection of recipes from the finest vegetarian restaurants in the country.

'One of the most useful books of the year. In fact there is such a good range of flavourings that the review copy is already looking very dog-eared.'
The Scotsman.

'A delightful book.' *BBC Radio.*

'A unique collection of recipes.' *Nottingham Evening Post.*

The Food & Wine Diary 1985—£2.95

A charming slimline pocket diary for the lover of food and wine. Filled with invaluable information, including charts on vintages, game seasons, fish seasons, a guide to London Restaurants, pages for tasting notes and much more. And throughout the main text of the diary a delightful mixture of quotations, anecdotes, illustrations, cartoons and serendip.
The perfect present for a gourmet's Christmas stocking.

If you would like to obtain any of the above titles they may be ordered through any bookshop or direct from Absolute Press, 14 Widcombe Crescent, Bath. BA2 6AH. Tel: 0225 316013. Please enclose a cheque or Postal Order for the correct amount plus 50 pence postage.